THE WISDOM OF BEES

THE WISDOM OF BEES

THE WISDOM OF BEES

WHAT THE HIVE CAN TEACH BUSINESS ABOUT LEADERSHIP, EFFICIENCY, AND GROWTH

Michael O'Malley, Ph.D.

Foreword by **Roxanne Quimby**,
Cofounder and Former CEO of Burt's Bees

PORTFOLIO

PORTFOLIO
Published by the Penguin Group
Penguin Group (USA) Inc., 375 Hudson Street, New York, New York 10014, U.S.A. •
Penguin Group (Canada), 90 Eglinton Avenue East, Suite 700, Toronto, Ontario, Canada
M4P 2Y3 (a division of Pearson Penguin Canada Inc.) • Penguin Books Ltd., 80 Strand,
London WC2R 0RL, England • Penguin Ireland, 25 St. Stephen's Green, Dublin 2, Ireland
(a division of Penguin Books Ltd) • Penguin Books Australia Ltd, 250 Camberwell Road,
Camberwell, Victoria 3124, Australia (a division of Pearson Australia Group Pty Ltd) •
Penguin Books India Pvt Ltd, 11 Community Centre, Panchsheel Park, New Delhi–110 017,
India • Penguin Group (NZ), 67 Apollo Drive, Rosedale, North Shore 0632, New Zealand
(a division of Pearson New Zealand Ltd) • Penguin Books (South Africa) (Pty) Ltd,
24 Sturdee Avenue, Rosebank, Johannesburg 2196, South Africa

Penguin Books Ltd, Registered Offices:
80 Strand, London WC2R 0RL, England

First published in 2010 by Portfolio,
a member of Penguin Group (USA) Inc.

10 9 8 7 6 5 4 3 2 1

Copyright © Michael O'Malley, 2010
All rights reserved

Library of Congress Cataloging-in-Publication Data

O'Malley, Michael, 1954–
The wisdom of bees : what the hive can teach business about leadership, efficiency, and
growth / Michael O'Malley ; foreword by Roxanne Quimby.
p.   cm.
Includes bibliographical references.
ISBN 978-1-59184-326-9
1. Organizational effectiveness.   2. Bees—Behavior.   3. Organizational
behavior.   4. Leadership.   5. Management.   I. Title.
HD58.9.O47 2010
658.4—dc22   2009050135

Printed in the United States of America
Set in Chaparral Pro with DIN
Designed by Daniel Lagin

To my brother-in-law Bill Samples of Honeymoon Apiaries,
who inspired this book through his gift of bees

CONTENTS

LESSONS FROM THE HIVE

LESSON 1
Protect the Future

LESSON 2
Keep Energy Levels Up

LESSON 3
Let Merit Be Your Guide

LESSON 4
Promote Community, Sanction Self-Interest

ILLUSTRATIONS

Michael O'Malley's intriguing analogy between business organizations and beehives provides delightful entertainment and clear instruction, which can be appreciated by businesspeople and laymen alike. In twenty-five brief chapters, the reader will come to understand how and why an enterprise succeeds or fails, using the imagery and science of bees at work for guidance.

As a businesswoman and former beekeeper, I can attest to the usefulness of this comparative model. O'Malley outlines a practical interpretation of bee productivity, division of labor, and the important role played by the queen bee (CEO). Free of personal agendas, each individual bee works closely and smoothly without cult of personality, jealousy, or infighting. Each has a role to play, including the natural leadership role of the queen-mother of the hive. In our business world, the female CEO is still a rarity, but I hope the day will come when we follow the example of the beehive and create opportunities for female leadership in a genderless business environment.

The reader will take great pleasure in O'Malley's readable metaphorical account in which he describes best practices in business based on his thoughtful analysis of the bee world—and his twenty-five-plus years as an organizational consultant. After you read this book, I assure you that you will never think about your organization in quite the same way. For me, as chief executive, the hives were an inspirational, ever-present reminder of the natural possibilities of organizational excellence. This wonderful book brings the world of the honeybee to life and, in so doing, shows what great organizations are capable of accomplishing.

Consider this book an encore performance by the great masters of efficiency, the honeybees, who through the author's pen will showcase what makes organizations effective. L. L. Langstroth, the man who invented the modern beehive, may have said it best in his *Langstroth's Hive and the Honey-Bee*: "The Creator may be seen in all the works of his hands; but in few more directly than in the wise economy of the honey-bee."

The Wisdom of Bees is charming, humorous, and, above all, unforgettably informative.

Enjoy!

—Roxanne Quimby
Cofounder and former CEO of Burt's Bees
July 1, 2009

My brother-in-law Bill, an accountant by day and tinkerer by night, came to town seven years ago. When he visits, it is like a New Age ancient bringing fire to the barbarians: there is always something new in store for us. Plus, he fixes doors that won't close, computers that run too slowly, and appliances that have lost a critical function.

On this particular trip, Bill told us about his newest hobby: beekeeping. He had installed forty hives, which is more than an enthusiast's pastime, but for us he espoused the benefits of having just one. Not only do these tiny creatures fascinate, he assured us, but the honey harvest in the fall is a sweet reward for their care. In addition, he continued, the relatively large, stingless male drones make wonderful, attention-grabbing specimens at show-and-tell and would be certain to transform our youngest child from an ordinary kid to, yes, a star.

Our impressionable ten-year-old son and I, his impressionable fortysomething father, were taken by these arguments and imagined the thrills that lay ahead. The wary ladies of the household, my fifteen-year-old daughter and my wife, were experienced in these episodes of whimsy. While they usually became willing accomplices to these schemes, they also were more questioning about such practicalities as "Who will take care of the bees?" Their suspicions about new pets were well grounded, as they recalled our recent misadventures with an escaped ball python (that my mother-in-law inadvertently found for us—but that is another story) and a seriously ill-tempered and stinky water turtle (Philbert) that my son and I bought while my wife was out of town.

Bill promised to make our entry into this new hobby an easy one. He would order both the hive and the gentle Italian honeybees. He would coach us through the preparation and assembly of the hive from afar and tell us how to handle the bees once we received them through the mail. Actually, bees go wherever the queen is, so getting them into the hive is easy. But my daughter and I had a mishap loading ants into an ant farm years before, so we had our concerns.

The parts to our hive arrived as scheduled, and we erected, painted, and placed it in a carefully selected, sheltered location in our backyard. As the delivery date for our bees approached, however, we realized that we had not notified our neighbors of our plans or properly gained their consent. We are fortunate to have kind and inquisitive neighbors to each side of us, but they had small children and we began to worry about how they would respond to the addition of fifty thousand members to our family.

As it happens, the neighbors greeted the news warmly and believed that having a hive in the neighborhood offered a great learning lab for the kids. One neighbor used this as an ideal time to let us know they were thinking of building a bat house on their roof. Well, our experiences with bats had not been very good since the night my wife nudged me awake to "something flying around the room." Let's just say the evening's resolution involved a yellow raincoat, a racquetball racquet, a bewildered child, a leaping dog, wrong numbers, and the police—and leave it at that. None of the neighbors thought bats were such a great idea, but we got thumbs-up on the bees.

This time we got it right.

THE WISDOM OF BEES

We have a stone bench in our backyard five feet from the entrance to our beehive. It is the perfect place to sit and watch the bees congregate on their front porch and to monitor their takeoffs and landings. Occasionally a flight path takes them in the direction of the bench, but the bees rapidly turn upward and dissolve into the sky. My head, like the head of a Pez dispenser, tilts back to see them off and then snaps back down to locate and track another bee preparing for its next mission.

It was during one of these observational episodes that this book was born. Sit around and watch the bees long enough and you notice the regularity of their behavior—the cadences and patterns—as well as their many seemingly premeditated encounters with one another when coming and going from the hive. It isn't obvious at first, but look hard at the hive and what you begin to notice most is the bees' organic artistry—a live performance and rendition of a Jackson Pollack drip painting. Their work suddenly makes sense.

When you watch the bees, sooner or later you just have to ask, How do they do it? How do thousands of bees working without reference to a specific blueprint manage to organize themselves in a meaningful way? What are they trying to achieve, how do they coordinate, and what makes them so successful? It seemed to me that the bees were working on the very same kinds of problems we are trying to solve in our organizations. How can large, diverse groups work together harmoniously and productively? I thought the bees could offer some helpful clues. Perhaps we could take what the bees do so well and apply it to our institutions so we can do better. It was a promising hypothesis and the beginning of this book.

We have had our bees for six years and there is no doubt they are a miracle of nature. They elicit a profound sense of awe in anyone who observes their industriousness in action. Foraging honeybees fly at fifteen miles per hour, flapping their wings at a ridiculously fast 230 beats per second, and cover an average territorial radius of one to two miles—but will travel as far as six to eight miles from the nest. Bees may gather as much as fifty pounds of nectar per day and produce two to three hundred pounds of honey per year (honey is regurgitated nectar that bees have concentrated to over 80 percent sugars by fanning their wings to evaporate excess water). One pound of honey requires fifty-five thousand miles of flight (one gallon requires one million miles) and the visitation of two million flowers. One teaspoon of honey represents the lifetime work of roughly a dozen bees (worker honeybees live, on average, six weeks—longer in winter). Known as the "angels of agriculture," bees also pollinate ninety major commercial crops, the equivalent of approximately $15 billion in agricultural production and one of every three mouthfuls of our food consumption.

Bees live in colonies with overlapping generations and do all of the things we do: provide shelter, care for their young, eat, work, and sleep. In addition, they have developed a system that rivals ours in complexity and surpasses it in efficiency. After all, they have had plenty of time to refine their organization. The oldest known bee is 100 million years old. It recently was found encased and preserved in amber within the Hukawng Valley in Myanmar. Scientists have speculated that bees evolved alongside flowering plants that were taking root during the Cretaceous era and may have begun their evolutionary journey out of Africa as long as 300 million years ago as a splinter group from wasps. This temporal progression represents a substantial head start on the relative newbies of the planet, *Homo sapiens*. And who wants to bet who will still be around in 100 million years?

The allegorical use of bees as a window into the management of our own social organizations may appear on first impression to be a stretch. For instance, it is tempting to presume that bees are hardwired, or programmed, in ways that we are not, and that our consciousness sets us apart in the animal kingdom. However, this either overstates the prowess of our species or underestimates the true abilities of the bee. As it happens, honeybees have two notable qualities that make them deserving of special attention: they communicate and they think. James Gould, in *The*

Animal Mind, went so far as to attribute consciousness to bees. We assume conscious decision making, for example, when we advise friends about restaurants based on factors such as quality, distance, and cost. Yet, when an energetic creature enclosed in an exoskeleton makes similar suggestions to her pals about flowers, we are reluctant to give them the same mental credit.

Bees are the only nonvertebrate animal (animal without a backbone) that has symbolic language. Because of bees' sophisticated forms of communication, some scientists have christened them "honorary mammals." In fact, bees have at least seventeen different, discrete communication signals (including their famous dance language) that use all of their senses. They even have their own version of an intranet built into their comb through which they transmit signals between 230 and 270 Hz. Bees have honed an exceptionally complex system of information exchange by which they monitor internal and external conditions, convey hive status and needs to one another, and direct activities.

If someone called me a "bee brain," I would take that as a compliment. Despite having a brain the size of a grass seed and blessed with only 950,000 neurons, bees have tremendous cognitive abilities. The highly integrated circuitry of the bee brain gives them the cognitive versatility they need to adapt as circumstances change. To be successful, honeybees, like us, have to be able to deviate from prescribed behaviors in order to meet environmental trials and unpredictable challenges.

Bees truly are small marvels. They can count (up to four) and recognize faces. They can categorize visual stimuli and form abstract rules of "same" and "different." They can spontaneously recall information and have a robust working memory that enables them to temporarily store, and patch together, multiple pieces of sensory information. If bees had cell phones, they could talk and fly at the same time without incident.

Bees travel many miles to and from the hive using celestial cues, local landmarks, and basic geometry to guide them. Bees view the world in color, can recognize shapes and patterns, and are responsive to a wide range of odors. They can visit up to ten thousand flowers in a day and accurately report places of interest to other bees. They can store and retrieve data about when and where to find high-quality, high-quantity resources, and adjust their behaviors accordingly. For example, they may have dandelions for a hearty breakfast, marjoram for lunch, and viper's bugloss for an early dinner.

These are complex critters with amazing intellectual capacities. Even seemingly simple abilities such as color recall are more difficult than you might think. For example, I have trouble going to the garden center and buying the same color impatiens that I had bought the day before. A bee would have no problem with this errand involving a simple matching task because they are able to discriminate among alternative colors a day after a onetime exposure of just one hundred milliseconds. To be sure, genetic programming underlies bees' behavioral feats. However, as is true of us, if bees were not given natural license to decide and act as conditions dictate, they would have long ago lost representation on Earth. Bees can think and communicate, and that makes the study of their social system particularly fascinating and compelling.

Bees have been revered by past generations who saw in the life of the hive virtues that were worthy of importing into our own society. From the honorific scribbling of cave dwellers, through the creation stories of the Egyptians and Greeks, to the biblical lands flowing with milk and honey; from Celtic revelry under the honey moon, to the coats of arms of the Middle Ages adorned with the courageous bee, to the utopian goo of the nineteenth century, the bee has been a divine emissary of the sacred and profound. In fact, through the millennia, bees at one time or another have come to symbolize power, health, immortality, wisdom, valor, eloquence, and plenty. These ready associations were not lost on demagogues such as Napoléon, who, when crowned emperor in 1804, dispensed with the traditional imperial garb in favor of a bee-studded coronation robe. However, his vision of the hive—and for his reign—was not one of community and democracy. Napoléon was seizing the grandeur of the bee for his own ends, and slyly legitimizing the occasion of his crowning—as in the hive, there will be a monarch.

Bees have rubbed shoulders with us for a very long time, giving and taking mythic powers through the relationship, both inspiring us from one generation to the next and serving as an instrument for our own ambitions. Within the hive dwells all that we have admired and worshipped through the ages—the heroic and resolute bee that productively conducts its affairs within a devoted community. It is the one social animal that lets us get close and allows us to observe the beauty and elegance of its motions. The bees quietly do their thing, and we commend them for it.

There is much to admire about the common honeybee. The honeybees' large accomplishments are especially impressive given their diminutive size. The clues to their success are to be found in their clever social organization that, in the words of Sherlock Holmes, "provides as much incident as can be found on the streets of London." Recall that Sherlock Holmes ultimately retires to Sussex Downs to live the reflective life of a beekeeper and to complete his magnum opus, *The Practical Handbook of Bee Culture*. When he is later brought back into service to capture the German spy von Bork, Watson is surprised by Holmes's reappearance, thinking that he had withdrawn from society. Holmes eases Watson's concerns by asserting that he has been fully engaged in the details of human interaction by spending many "pensive nights and laborious days" watching the "little workings of gangs."

As both an organizational consultant and beekeeper for many years, I can concur with the always-astute Inspector Holmes that nature has laid before us a wondrous template from which to learn. The "little gangs" that will serve as our model throughout this book come from the genus and species *Apis mellifera*: translated "the honey-bearing bee." These bees are known for their highly social colonies and hexagonal wax cells. The honeybees we mostly see in our backyards are of European ancestry and scientifically known as *ligustica*.

The honeybee has mastered a great society and it would be phylogenic hubris to think we have nothing to learn from them. To paraphrase Shakespeare (*The Tempest*), they are the magistrates, merchants, and soldiers that teach the art of order to a peopled kingdom. Thus, using the evolutionary wisdom and operational excellence of honeybees as the model, I discuss twenty-five lessons that can be applied in any type of organization and at any organizational level to beneficial effect. Some of the lessons will sound familiar, and you can accept them as gentle reminders of their importance: principles you know to be true but perhaps to which you have not given sufficient emphasis in your organization. Other lessons may supply those rare missing pieces to complete organizational success.

I have sprinkled examples of the lessons throughout the text in order to highlight their organizational relevance. Nevertheless, since general lessons are meant to be . . . generalizable, I have left plenty of room for your imagination. Given that the range of possible colony-to-corporation translations is limitless, I did not see the logic of crowding out your ideas by overspecifying my own. Most of the time, you will readily grasp the organizational implications of honeybees' behavior. Nevertheless, I added further thoughts at the end of each chapter to stimulate your thinking about ways in which you might intervene in your organization. In the spirit of the beehive, I have labeled these closing paragraphs "More Pollen": protein supplements for the brain, as it were. The rationale behind this heading will become apparent as you read the book.

One way you might think about the twenty-five lessons is as a checklist by which you mark the degree to which your organization realizes the lessons, and whether a little more or a little less expression of each would be desirable. To assist you, I have provided a summary of the lessons at the end of the book on pages 189–194, formatted in a way you can easily scan and flag for further consideration.

I ordered the lessons in the main text to introduce you gradually to the honeybee, beginning with basic information and building from there. There is nothing preventing you from skipping from chapter to chapter if that is how you prefer to read. There are a few facts you will encounter in later chapters that presume some understanding of what came before, but you would get the gist of the material. In the concluding chapter, I discuss the lessons according to the type of competing demands to which the honeybees are trying to cope. These opposing forces, or dilemmas, provide a shorthand way to encode all of the lessons, making it easier to retrieve their significance in the context of your work.

Second, the concept of a hive provides a systemic way of conceptualizing the workplace and your institutional strategies and operations. The lessons set forth collectively reflect the honeybees' best case for the management of a productive society. If you stopped and asked yourself, How can my organization survive and grow while wasting as little energy and resources as possible? the answer would be the twenty-five lessons. As you look for ways to improve your organization, it would not be outlandish to take a step back and ask yourself, What would a bee do?

In fact, I recently rhetorically posed this question to the management of a customer response center. A call center is a lot like the bees of a hive who await the return of incoming foragers—callers—who need help unloading their nectar. As you will see, the colony's operations quickly change based on one critical measure: the length of time it takes foragers to find the help they seek from receivers. This observation presented an ideal starting place for a discussion of how the call center might organize in order to improve responsiveness to callers.

The science presented in the book is straightforward. No experience is required. Unless I note otherwise, the lessons are based on what researchers currently believe to be true about honeybees. If you happen to fall for these lovely creatures as you learn more about them, I have provided a bibliography to further your exploration. Everything I mention about bees is contained in the books and articles I list. The bibliography also includes citations to the newspaper and magazine articles I mention in the text.

Unfairly reputed, as they are, to be hardened aggressors who sting without provocation or annoying party crashers at summer outings, it is time to freshen the honeybee's image. My hope is that the next time you spot a bee you will instantly think, "Remarkable creature," and consider what they quietly teach through the lessons of the hive.

LESSONS FROM THE HIVE

LESSON 1

PROTECT THE FUTURE

The Belgian-born Nobel laureate in literature Maurice Maeterlinck once commented, "The God of the bee is the future." Everything the bee does employs this orientation as the basis for its actions; what is done today is always in anticipation of tomorrow. Indeed, the tendency for action to be in the context and service of the future is so central that it belongs as our first lesson.

I am almost embarrassed to discuss this lesson since its benefit to business leaders seems self-evident. Nevertheless, it may be a hopeful message for those executives who feel enslaved by quarterly earnings reports. And we could ask the subprime lenders and the lineup of insurers, packagers, and distributors of those mortgages responsible for the most recent banking crisis if they were thinking of the long term when they took on so much risk. Or we could ask auto manufacturers if concentrating on trucks and sport utility vehicles for earnings was truly advisable. Unlike these companies, however, bees are not short-term maximizers. Instead, honeybees' basic strategy is to maximize returns over a broad geographic area and extended time horizon.

Bees don't focus exclusively on the most productive flower patches at any given time, and for good reason. Conditions change rapidly for bees and they can ill afford wide swings in pollen and nectar intake. What is best now probably won't be tomorrow. In the animal kingdom, the "famine" in "feast or famine" is a death sentence. Thus, when a lucrative vein of nectar is discovered, the entire colony doesn't rush off to mine it no matter how enriching the short-term benefits. The colony has internalized a very important natural rule: someday the nectar in that location will stop flowing and they will need to be prepared to rapidly reallocate resources to other productive sites. In order to do so, they must already know where those sites are and have established operations, however minimal, in those locales. Said succinctly, bees avoid all-or-none scenarios at all costs.

The work of bees is daunting when you consider the fickle ecological conditions they encounter within a territory of a multimile radius. The season, the weather, the time of day, the types of flowers, and the competition for nectar with birds and other insects all are important considerations for successful foraging. Given the highly volatile environment, concentrating inordinate amounts of resources in one place for too long would be a disastrous mistake. Under these conditions, bees give up immediate rewards for longer-term adaptation within an immense terrain where incomplete information is the norm. They harvest and search simultaneously with the purpose of extracting the greatest benefit over a protracted time span. Operationally, this produces a pattern among bees in which they monitor a large area but differentially focus on a limited number of sites at any given time that are the most profitable. In the language of business, bees are heavily invested in research and development, constantly on the lookout for the next best thing while taking in revenues from available sources.

This argues for companies to allocate a percentage of their available resources to new goods and markets, and to concepts at various stages of development to replace aging products or outdated services. This includes maintaining investment levels even when there is the temptation to pull back in times of scarcity. Actually, if you follow what the bees do, you would expand exploration during low-growth periods. The number of scout bees that seek out new sources of wealth for the colony actually increases as available forage declines. As conditions worsen, honeybees ratchet up their search. In fact, that's what many innovative R&D-dependent companies such as 3M, Intel, Procter & Gamble, and Xerox have done in the past in order to fill their product pipelines and expand into new markets and businesses. Minimally, these companies do all they can to safeguard R&D expenditures using something akin to what Corning calls a "rings of defense" strategy with investment dollars nestled in the protective core.

The problems many companies face are a result of a temporal mirage. Motivated by an extreme thirst for profits, they fail to see that the source of plenty eventually disappears. Quenched by easy money and luscious margins, they overindulge and underexplore, disregarding that it all will pass. Frequently businesses that are enjoying rich harvests in fields of plenty fail to notice the shrinkage and decay around the edges, and the promising, budding sprouts in their neighbor's yard. If bees settled around the one best food source available within a particular period, the resulting allocation of labor would be too concentrated on a single site. As the profitability of the site dwindled—which it inevitably would—the time it would take to search for and harvest the next patch would create a period in which there was no yield whatsoever.

More Pollen

The best way to ensure that there will be a short run is to focus on the long run. This may take some convincing of those who see it the other way around, such as shareholders. However, as the bees clearly advise through their behavior, overexploiting a rich patch just because it is there is a death trap. In this regard, why make it harder on yourself by creating organizational structures such as pay plans that reward short-term feasts?

Good companies are durable over the long run and require continued investment in good times and bad. Coarse reductions in exploratory spending constrict future market options and erode a company's entrepreneurial edge. Innovation is not like a switch that can be turned off and on at will. It requires experience, knowledge acquisition, and trial and error. In a phrase, innovation requires *continuity of learning*, which is grossly interrupted when critical initiatives are indefinitely put on hold. The negative effects of excessive cuts and overexploitation persist well after organizations experience a change of heart and hurriedly attempt to make amends. Regardless of your relative position in the organization, the less people are pressed to experiment, learn, and grow, the less inventive your people will be when eventually called upon to try something new.

LESSON 2

KEEP ENERGY LEVELS UP

If you ran one mile as fast as you could, how quickly could you then run a second? A one-mile sprint makes sense only if when you cross the finish line you are finished. However, we humans have to get up in the morning, as do bees, and get ourselves to work day after day. Bees are careful to conserve their precious fuel during the hunt and harvest of resources in order to avoid depleting themselves. In the course of their recurring service, bees never compromise the long-term success of the organization by exhausting their capacity to perform.

Bees evaluate the quality of a food source by its net value to the hive, not simply by the total nectar they can collect. This is because collecting involves the expenditure of costly energy. Gathering nectar and pollen is both dangerous and wearing, and ultimately reduces the efficiency and life span of the foraging forces. Like the treads on tires, bees' wings do not last forever. Bees, then, aren't indifferent to two identical food sources located at different distances from the hive. All else being equal, they will prefer the closer patch. They also consider other variables as they harvest, such as the distance between flowers and the sugar concentration of the nectar.

The lesson, then, is that businesses should not expect employees to repeatedly run back-to-back miles and simultaneously expect that the company will be able to maintain the same level of productivity. Many executives will say, "We don't do that. If anything, we expect too little from our employees." But that isn't always true. Companies can run their workforces into the proverbial ground in all sorts of ways. I'll mention just a few that I frequently address when conferring with companies on work flow and organizational design.

First, work rules—whether in unionized environments or not—often assign the most difficult or heaviest work to the greenest members of the institution. Retail salespeople with the least tenure are scheduled for the hours in which there is greatest activity. Similarly, new entrants into warehouses tend to do all of the heavy lifting without relief from coworkers who have advanced to less taxing jobs.

Second, many companies mechanically apply revenue increases as a part of their budget processes and five-year plans without first considering other organizational factors that will need adjusting, such as staffing levels and business processes. The result is that too few people using inadequate or outdated methods struggle to keep pace with new demands for increased output. What's more, as output increases and companies become more complex, organizations frequently introduce new red tape, and checks and balances that make the old-fashioned ways in which the work was performed more grueling.

Third, a few companies simply try to wring out every drop of productivity from employees until they are emotionally and physically exhausted. These businesses view workers as replaceable units, displaying a marked indifference to the welfare of their employees and customers. The bizarre work practices within the United States' commuter airline industry provide a ready example. In general, the relatively low-paid pilots of regional carriers often commute far distances to their airline hubs for duty (often more than four hundred miles), but their time clocks don't start until they report in as a crew member. The resulting pilot fatigue has been cited by oversight organizations as a factor in commuter airline crashes.

When people tire out, they tire in different ways. Some call in sick, others slow their work pace, become increasingly lax in the delivery of service, or make mistakes. A few become aggressive and confrontational. And some just drop out through voluntary turnover. Moreover, just when you need them to rally, they will lack the energy to gather the nectar and pollen equivalents a company needs. So, while CEOs can be pumping up sales and pleasing analysts in the short run, they may be systematically destroying the long-term value of the company.

More Pollen

A key principle of organizational development is to preserve the future ability of a company to perform. Honeybees succeed at this by being smart about how they gather nectar. They are not indiscriminate revenue chasers. Rather, they factor in the costs of collection for maximum production at minimum expenditure of energy. As a manager, you might want to survey your own work group for conditions that stretch employees too thin for too long.

Corporations can be potentially tiring, routine places that wear people down over time. While it is not feasible for an employee to be "on" every day, companies can cultivate strong performances by inspired job designs that reduce the repetitive nature of certain kinds of work while adding elements that are stimulating and thought provoking. It takes imagination and managerial attentiveness, but all positions can be meaningfully expanded in ways that add variety and challenge. Other ways to nourish and renew employees include: sabbaticals, special assignments, seminars with interesting colleagues, provision for independent study—anything that suspends business as usual in favor of invigorating, growth-related experiences. Periodic restorative breaks are like tune-ups that reengage employees' mental faculties, awaken their creative instincts, and keep organizations vital.

WHEN COLONIES AND COMPANIES DIE YOUNG

A few years ago, I examined the turnover of sales personnel for a major department store by tracking cohorts of workers from the time they entered the company until they voluntarily exited. I showed executives that their company was replacing every worker three times per year to keep the workforce at a steady state. They had not realized the dimensions of the problem, although they knew they had one. In order to fill vacancies, recruiters accepted every warm body that walked through the door and trainers whisked new hires through orientation; the results were mounting customer complaints and declining revenues. The stores were clearly trapped in a self-defeating loop traceable to the employee turnover rate. The high turnover rate generated conditions that put inordinate pressure on the company to bring new people into the organization but, at the same time, poorly equipped them to be effective at their stations. If the company wanted to be successful, it would have to increase the average longevity of its workforce.

If bees experienced an equivalent rate of loss to this department store, the hive would be doomed. As at the retail store, the significant turnover of bees would necessarily refocus colony efforts on the birthing and nurturing (on-boarding) of new bees, with the consequential loss of experienced frontline foragers and disruption in gathering and storing product. The result would be deterioration in colony fitness. *Hives with longer colony life spans are more effective and more successful.*

Honeybees have a control point known as the age at first

forage (AFF). It is the average time bees leave the hive to become foragers. Once out of the hive, honeybees live about another one to two weeks. Ideally, the AFF of the hive will stay within a range that keeps the average life expectancy of the colony in balance with foraging effectiveness. That is, the AFF is set to balance the development time needed for the bees to mature with a productive life span in the field. Colonies that are forced by circumstances (that is, they need foragers fast) to hasten brood production and developmental periods (in essence, move the AFF forward in time) end up like our retailer—they spend too much energy bringing in new bodies who die young in the field because they aren't ready, physiologically or experientially. Many of the hives caught in this cycle will fail.

Companies are most vulnerable to employee defections soon after employees are hired and for roughly the ensuing two years—following employees' initial and formative experiences with the company. Just as the honeybee colony needs to keep the AFF at a logistically safe place, companies need to keep what might be called their DOC—day of commitment— at a healthy place. Companies need to convince employees that they made the right choice early in their tenure, so that turnover rates flatten sooner and people stay longer. The longer people stay, the quicker the company can step off a reproductive treadmill and more fully attend to the generative lives of its workers. All relationships begin with some lingering uncertainties; the sooner employees and employers agree that they were meant for each other, the happier and more productive they all will be.

LESSON 3

LET MERIT BE YOUR GUIDE

Honeybee colonies are meritocracies. Unlike the institutions with which we are familiar, favoritism plays little role in the operations of the hive. The smooth, efficient functioning of the hive trumps preservation of an individual's genetic lineage. There are no competitive struggles among familial cliques of bees to displace coordination across the colony. This selfless aspect of bees makes them atypical in the natural world and a eusocial insect—a species in which individuals altruistically forsake their reproductive potential for the good of the group (only the queen has the natural right to reproduce).

In general, anything that potentially interferes with colony efficiency is selectively disfavored. Put simply, bees cannot afford to play favorites. The same, of course, cannot be said of our tendency to allow friendship ties and feelings of reciprocity to affect our better judgments. Arguably, these qualities distinguish our humanity, but work assignments, pay increases, and job promotions that are based on internal

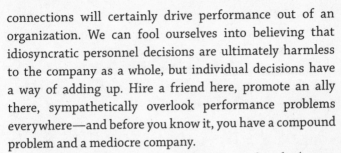
connections will certainly drive performance out of an organization. We can fool ourselves into believing that idiosyncratic personnel decisions are ultimately harmless to the company as a whole, but individual decisions have a way of adding up. Hire a friend here, promote an ally there, sympathetically overlook performance problems everywhere—and before you know it, you have a compound problem and a mediocre company.

Conspicuously, the ruler of the hive is female (as are most of her subjects, the worker bees). Science took a very long time to come to grips with this fact. Even as evidence of a feminine monarchy within the hive grew throughout the seventeenth and eighteenth centuries, attempts were made to fit the new discoveries into the framework of the prevailing attitudes on class and gender. The newly crowned queen of the honeybees was assigned a host of matronly qualities. She was described as a gentle, merciful, and loving bee that remained virtuously chaste. As it happens, none of this is true; queens have retractable and reusable stingers they readily use to secure power and have many suitors and mates. Indeed, the promiscuous queen carries the sperm of twelve to fifteen males on average.

Eventually, good science during the Enlightenment over-came the prejudices of the era with scientists concluding that nature favors what works as opposed to what we want to believe. Among honeybees, females have the preeminent role in tending to the health and survival of the hive. There are no wax ceilings in the hive. What matters most is who best can promote the welfare and longevity of the colony.

The effects of the performance-oriented society of bees

extend to the queen herself. When the productivity of the queen diminishes, that is, as her egg-laying capacities wane, she is replaced by a more able heir. An average reign is roughly two to three years. The fundamental emphasis on contribution filters throughout the hive. More vigorous and productive bees recurrently replace the ranks of aging workers.

In addition, honeybees show little tolerance for the male drones once their services to the hive are no longer needed. The drones are studly, powerful fliers who boldly chase after the queen during treacherous mating flights. Those who succeed die in an aerial free fall. Those who fail return to the hive, hang out, and enjoy occasional, leisurely flights on sunny afternoons. However, as winter approaches and the hive must live off its fixed store of honey for several months, those who feast on this golden nectar but who do not contribute to the group become expendable. Now well past their prime and incapable of being rehabilitated into another colony role, drones who have not yet died from natural causes are unceremoniously tossed out of the hive by workers in a daylong event known as the "massacre of the drones." Since drones, unlike workers, do not have stingers, cleaning house is a decisive, one-sided affair. This all occurs quickly and matter-of-factly when the cost of carrying dead wood becomes too great. When the time comes for swift action, there is no mistaking the criterion used in determining who stays and who goes: the level of contribution to the group. When it comes to merit, the dictum of honeybees is "If you want to eat the honey, you must contribute to the hive": a

reasonable admonishment to anyone in the corporate world charged with getting results.

When I have asked executives about their biggest mistakes, they list being slow to act on personnel issues among the top three. Against their better judgments, they tolerated inferior performance or disruptive people for too long. On the other hand, we can appreciate decisive leaders such as Carol Bartz, who as CEO of Autodesk and Yahoo! demonstrated an ability to distill complex technology companies to their serviceable essence and to make hard, unsentimental choices about which people and assets belong in the corporation. This doesn't mean that the workplace should be stripped of compassion, only that compassion—or the avoidance of conflict—should not jeopardize the welfare of the group. Overall, the more that merit is corrupted by factors unrelated to performance, the worse off your organization will be.

More Pollen

Honeybees are performance-centric. Relationship ties and good-ole-girl networks are insignificant in the conduct of the colony. What's more, performance is built into the institutional fabric of the hive with no special accommodation for a year-end review—that loathsome, annual, organizational ritual that undermines the very thing it is supposed to instill: motivation. Honeybees are constantly making consensus determinations of the queen's vitality and pruning and replacing members of the colony based on workers' capacity to perform. In broader organizational terms, it could be said that the hive has a strong culture of performance.

To lead like a bee, managers can similarly reinforce the centrality of performance by providing ongoing feedback and instruction; regularly gathering information from *capable* colleagues, customers, and others about employees' performances; and recognizing the exemplary performances of individuals and *teams* throughout the year. In these ways, performance remains a salient concern at the institutional forefront.

LESSON 4

PROMOTE COMMUNITY,
SANCTION SELF-INTEREST

Every day, millions of tiny decisions are made by employees throughout the corporate world. Many of these follow a similar form: "How much should I do for myself, and how much should I do for the company?" The results of these decisions are often reflected in economic reports on lost time and productivity. Most decisions that weigh in on the self-interested side of the ledger occur infrequently and are reasonably harmless when averaged over time: incidental moonlighting, an extra "precautionary" sick day, a modestly extended lunch, and a slighter slower pace on the shop floor.

Corporate problems mount, however, as the frequency and size of self-interest climb: the employee who withholds breakthrough ideas in order to keep them for himself someday; the self-aggrandizing leader who makes questionable acquisitions because it makes him feel good about himself; the self-indulgent rogue trader who brings his financial institution to its knees through large, risky trading positions.

The riddle of what's mine and what's yours is neatly settled by the bees. The organizing theme of the hive is that everything is done for the good of the whole, and the community is central to the operations of the colony. As a true social system, every bee works and sacrifices to produce an organization that is greater than the sum of the parts. For example, unlike the occasions when I have taken my kids berry picking, the pollen and nectar that the bees collect isn't half gone by the time they get back to the hive. The bees forgo immediate gratification for the sake of the group by delivering and unloading their entire cargo only once they have returned to the hive. In contrast to the marauding, independent "lone wolves" of corporations who are tolerated as long as they are useful, there are no "lone bees" in the colony and it is preposterous to imagine a honeybee living a solitary life outside of the hive.

Companies that are unable to build community cannot succeed over the long run. The more employees have internalized the values of the organization, the more likely it is that the organization will thrive. The personal work goals of employees within a company must not only be aligned with the goals of the institution, they must be the same. The honeybee toils on behalf of the group, with the group's interests as her own.

Shared values, which are instilled through frequent messages as well as the demonstrable behaviors of managers, serve as the social glue in organizations. Communal work becomes easier to perform when a company frames its

activities within the context of a higher purpose or mission that is viewed as a worthy pursuit. But keeping people together and delaying immediate personal rewards for the sake of the group's welfare are no easy tasks. Communication, modeling, and reinforcement of desirable behaviors are helpful beginnings but no panacea.

Cooperation is hard to sustain even in the beehive. There are circumstances in which the temptation for self-interest is high and must be suppressed. Cooperation does not occur automatically in human or bee societies. It would be nice if everyone recognized the wisdom of collective action and the advantages derived from it, but free-rider problems will likely be with us forever.

What can we learn about how hives manage their share of internal discord? The bees' strategy involves something analogous to a police force, which, in their case, is responsible for controlling unwanted births of male offspring. Only a tiny fraction of female worker bees have functional ovaries and are capable of laying eggs, but these eggs will only develop into males (unfertilized eggs become males). While these female workers are undoubtedly motivated by natural reproductive desires, a hive full of drones would be a very bad idea indeed. Producing too many males would require significant investment in reproductive care without recognizing any corresponding value to colony maintenance and efficiency.

The state of affairs in which self-interest prevails is so disastrous to the well-being of the hive that it has appropriately been called "anarchy." Drones can perform only one task, inseminating the queen, and only so many drones are needed. Consequently, the colony has certain bees (essentially those who are incapable of laying eggs) that are on the lookout for violators, both preventing harm through their vigilance and correcting social wrongs by destroying eggs that have been laid.

The idea of a roaming police force seems a bit much when applied to corporations, implying a level of oversight that is too oppressive. Rather, policing in organizations should be interpreted more modestly as an unwillingness to tolerate those who are only out for themselves and whose behaviors, if allowed, would have a destructive effect on the overall organization. "Group welfare" should not become a managerial excuse to deny all personal requests for more people, financial resources, or space. As a leader, however, you must be able to set a limit to requests or behaviors that cross the boundary from the well-intentioned to the it's-all-about-me variety.

Many studies on animals and humans have shown that high levels of cooperation are achievable over the long run only if group members are willing and able to rein in those who act out of self-interest. That is, in order to stabilize cooperative behaviors as the norm in the long term, members of the group must be willing to thwart the more self-indulgent individuals in the short term. In colonies, the queen sends chemical messages that foster self-restraint in egg laying among the workers—basically highlighting the rule of law through her communications—but these aren't completely effective unless reinforced locally through policing. Building a strong community, then, requires that a manager emphasize desirable behaviors *and* display a readiness to sanction behaviors that are in conflict with the cooperative interests of the group. Cooperation cannot be effectively regulated through positive reinforcement alone.

Game theorists use a simulation in which people need to collectively organize in order to achieve their objective. The simulation is called "stag" and serves as an apt representation of what goes on in organizations when violations of community norms go unchecked. In order to catch a stag, a group has to surround it in unison. If some members within the group are "no-shows" because they have better things to do, the stag escapes. Now, if I am a member of a group and believe that there will in fact be no-shows, then what would be the use of my participation? You see the problem. If cooperation isn't enforced, then collective action breaks down into a mire of everyone-for-themselves. Although no one wants to be in an organization in which there is widespread disaffection, no one wants to be the dupe who tries to catch the stag alone either. The stag will still escape and the company or the project will still fail.

The positive and influential role of leadership must not be underestimated in the discussion above. In fact, without a queen, the entire social order unravels rather quickly. The prized cooperative value system falls apart. Policing ceases, egg laying of workers increases, and the colony—unable to produce a replacement queen—dies. In the absence of the queen, it is as if each worker vies for control and tries to assume authority over the hive by producing offspring of her own. It is an effort doomed for failure. Solitary pursuits rapidly displace community and sacrifice in a final spasm of cultural unrest and organizational decay.

However, reintroduce the leader-queen, and purposeful behavior resumes. It is like raising the royal standard over Buckingham Palace—there is a pervasive sense of comfort knowing that the Queen is in and all is well within the kingdom. A strong, positive culture requires strong leadership. In those situations when people do not play by the rules, the leader must step in to underscore the value of community.

More Pollen

Cooperation and unified action require deliberate, ongoing attention. As our personal experiences can attest, smooth teamwork is not automatic. Good ideas that emerge from healthy tensions within groups are fine. What is not okay, however, is for people to extract the benefits of association for their personal advantage. The bees show a readiness to sanction members of the hive that break with the community to pursue their own reproductive potential. Moreover, the honeybees don't wait until the problems associated with self-interest have hatched and spread before intervening. If they see workers laying eggs, they stop them. If they find eggs that have been laid, they destroy them. They act quickly to make sure the social order of the hive is preserved. As a manager, engaging in remedial actions sooner rather than later will generally save you from bigger messes down the road.

Importantly, managers should reinforce the enterprise-wide community and not local communities scattered about the organization. Foragers don't have one community and nurse bees another, for example. Take a clue from the bees and consider the following two ways to build a wide sense of community and camaraderie. First, move people around the organization a little, allowing them to cross departmental lines when feasible—all bees during their lifetimes do several jobs across castes. Second, create cross-disciplinary teams or organize work in a way that makes outcomes an obvious by-product of collaborations among different functional groups—bees work in close proximity and constantly and reciprocally trade resources and information (I will say more about this throughout the book).

LESSON 5

DISTRIBUTE AUTHORITY

The honeybee colony operates through decentralized authority. Bees make daily decisions about taking out the trash or feeding the young based on local cues and requirements. Certain bees are simply in a better position to assess the needs of the colony at any particular moment and to stimulate action based on their direct experiences. Bees show us, then, an alternative to bureaucratic controls that can stifle action and discourage employee initiative. Too often, managers insist on making decisions for which they do not have all of the relevant information, and squash the decision-making abilities of those who do. In contrast, Railroad Associates Corp., an engineering and contracting concern, was selected as one of the top small workplaces in 2009 primarily because of the considerable authority it gives to frontline workers. In fact, the company does not even have a middle management layer. Instead, the company chooses to increase employee know-how through on-the-job training, on-site mentoring, and formal coursework, and to provide employees with timely access to critical data through quality informational systems. The goal is to give line workers the ability to solve problems on their own.

With many thousands of employed workers, the queen couldn't possibly direct all of the actions in the field from her command post. Besides, she's busy creating future generations. So, she does what every good leader does: she delegates certain responsibilities to a set of lead bees who act as agents for her majesty.

The queen produces a number of pheromones and esters in her mandibular glands, and blends of these chemicals are involved in important hive functions such as building comb. Some of the queen's directives are communicated through airborne transmission of her chemicals, but surface transport is highly likely as well. Court bees that attend to and groom the queen spread her chemical messages to other bees through surface-to-surface contact, who then further spread the queen's chemicals, and so on. Thus the queen's messages are distributed throughout the colony in an informational cascade that would be the envy of every corporate planner.

Indeed, goal setting is supposed to work in precisely this fashion, with the wishes of the CEO and her executive team rippling through the company and acted upon as intended. Nevertheless, the point is that the commands of neither the queen nor the CEO can be effectively dispersed without the aid of reliable messengers, starting with those who are closest to their respective leaders. Once the debates and discussions end, CEOs need to be surrounded by those who will diligently convey their directives.

While the queen is the genetic heart and soul of the hive,

she is by no means the only leader. Other bees in the hive act as supervisors who initiate activities. These key individuals serve as nodes in a social network or as informational centers around which performance is organized. Self-organizing—the process by which individual bees acting on unique information produce beneficial group results—is put into motion by lead bees. A classic example in honeybee colonies is the early-morning foragers who are the first to find food. They return to the nest, venture deep into the hive, and, with a shaking signal, rouse others to action by informing them that a productive period of activity is about to begin. It is a little like waking children for school each morning. It may appear that bees operate in isolation of leadership, but in fact the system is infused with motivators who kick-start action (interestingly, as in our society, some bees require bigger kicks than others to get moving).

Those tasked with responding to the transmitted needs of the colony do so diligently. Given that nature is unforgiving, just completing the job is not sufficient. The job must be done well. Accountability is crucial for the workers because colonies may not get a second chance.

Let's take swarming as an example. Successful hives can become so large in numbers that their size becomes unsustainable. In order to adapt, a subset of the hive leaves en masse. Approximately ten to fifteen thousand bees from the colony, joined by the old queen, leave the hive in search of a new home. These swarms appear as dense clouds of bees the size of soccer balls, the frightening-looking stuff of sci-fi films. It is, in fact, a wondrously chilling sight, but the bees' purpose is single-minded and their presence is benign.

The swarm quickly settles, hung like a gangly beard from a tree branch or similar resting spot. Hundreds of scout bees leave the swarm and scatter in search of a new home. Possible settlements will naturally vary but bees use a common set of criteria in evaluating sites. For example, bees prefer homes with a certain volume, entrance size, exposure, and height from the ground. Therefore, bees set out on their mission with clear guidelines of what constitutes success. They don't make it up as they go along—a due warning to anyone who starts a job without first defining its goals and parameters. In the bees' case, the goal is to find a new home, but not just any old home will do. They need one that keeps them out of harm's way and supports the colony's reproductive interests, and over many millions of years they have learned which dimensions matter most.

Most scouts return to the swarm without having found a site that satisfies minimum requirements. A dozen or so scouts return with good news. This news is expressed through the bees' dance language on the surface of the swarm. The higher the quality of the site, the more enthusiastic the dance. The purpose of the dance is to recruit uncommitted scouts to their site for a showing.

Uncommitted scouts can be either other scouts who did not find a suitable property or bees that abandon their initial selections and essentially become free agents. Scout bees repeatedly return to their chosen sites for additional looks, but their enthusiasm for the site declines at a relatively fixed rate with each visit. This means that bees' attraction to lower-quality hives extinguishes first, creating the opportunity for them to visit spots that are more seductive. In effect, bees abandon their initial positions and "reset" their commitment levels as they become open to new possibilities.

Recruits to a new site do not necessarily agree with a scout's initial assessment and may make repeated visits to this and other locations before committing. Thus the recruits serve as checks on first impressions and prevent bees from making deadly errors. As more and more scouts are attracted to a particular site and a quorum for that location is reached, the scout bees emit a high-pitched piping sound to inform the swarm that departure is imminent and to prepare themselves for the move. This is the near conclusion of a momentous life-or-death decision process that is entirely made by worker bees in the field, operating outside the control of a central authority.

The piping signal essentially tells the colony to start their engines. Bees have to warm their flight muscles by shivering before they can take off. The recruiting and decision process continues during this preparatory period, which takes about an hour, and when there is liftoff, the scouts usually have come to unanimous agreement regarding their new home. Total agreement or not, the decision has been made. In a sense, the time lag between a decision and liftoff allows the swarming colony to prepare for, and acclimate to, change. It is what we all need at times, a period of adjustment.

Two of the best indicators of a healthy decision process are the abilities of people to consider alternatives and to change their minds based on information that conflicts with their original position.

Vacating positions comes easily for bees since their evolutionary priority is to the colony. Organizations seek different objectives but must do so with the same aim of supplanting personal interests with organizational ones. What happens in your organization, however, when competing ideas are presented? Which ideas prevail, and why: power, somebody's turn to be right, personal pride and ambition? Often companies find it difficult to change from one decision pathway to another because personal agendas at the individual and departmental levels get in the way.

A part of good leadership is the ability to put personal motives aside for the sake of the company. And sometimes, good leadership means taking a step back. Let's think about all of this for a moment. What could the leader—the queen— add to the process of scouting for a new hive? Nothing! The only thing the leader can do in this case is get in the way. She doesn't have as much relevant information as the scouts, nor does she see the future more clearly. In the world of humans under similar circumstances, all the leader can do is repeat the questions that already have been asked and contemplated, and delay decisions through the contagion of anxiety. It is hard to let go but also necessary for a leader to ask, "Can my employees do the job, and will I let them do it?"

More Pollen

Those closest to the information should make the relevant decision. Decentralization is one of the hallmarks of the honeybee colony. Foraging decisions, for example, are made by the foragers. The information doesn't travel up to the queen and back down again. If you are thinking of shifting greater power away from the organizational core and into the field, however, consider these facts first: 1) bees have clear objectives; 2) they are excellent communicators and are able to quickly take in and consolidate information— and transform that information into coordinated action; and 3) they are reliable workers that are very good at what they do. "Empowerment" has developed a bad reputation in companies because it only has been halfway defined as pushing out decision-making authority. But that won't work without having the other half in place—clarity of goals, sound communications, the requisite talent, and such.

Minimally, I suggest you give team members the elbow room to be responsible by giving them some decision-making authority. When you give an assignment to someone, the best way to demonstrate that you care about the results and are counting on the person to come through is by discussing the resources that will be essential for the mission and by following up on progress. And never accept excuses for non-performance or allow the results of the assignment to slip by without notice. Sooner rather than later employees will get the point that you won't forget your request, that you are serious about it, and that you consider the work being done to be of organizational consequence.

When an unfulfilled task presents itself, an employee can think in one of two ways: "This is not my responsibility" or "This is my responsibility." Either assumption is easy to instill with sufficient training. Which would you prefer your employees reflexively make?

LESSON 6

MAKE GOOD ENOUGH DECISIONS

When bees leave their hive in search of a new home, they open themselves up to risks from weather and predators. As they wait to find the right place, they also are expending the small store of energy (sugar solution) they bring with them. This means that the bees must make decisions quickly in their hunt for a suitable location. Somewhere in the world is the perfect nest with ideal specifications. However, an exhaustive, costly search for Eldorado is not an option. A time comes in the decision process when the nominal gains and escalating costs associated with prolonged data gathering and analysis must yield to action. Even though the choice may not be optimal, the bees make a choice.

The monumental decision of honeybees is made in an arena in which imperfect information is the norm and there are no absolutes.

In management, we frequently believe that only one correct answer exists. However, this is seldom true, even in the simplest of matters. Even the answer to 1+1 is contestable. For example, combining equal parts of certain fluids does not equal twice as much liquid. Thus, in business and elsewhere, we have to overcome a lifetime of educational brainwashing that insists that answers are right or wrong rather than better or worse. A decision does not have to be perfect. The decision just has to be good. In the words of Eli Lilly's CEO John Lechleiter, "We need to act on 80 percent, not 99.5 percent, of the information."

As the bees instruct, "incomplete" information is not the same as "insufficient" information. Bees take two precautions to ensure that the adequacy of a decision is not a victim to the speed with which the choice is made. These precautions are consistent with the assumptions embedded in the "collective wisdom" theorem advanced by the French intellectual Marquis de Condorcet in the eighteenth century. He showed that larger groups almost always make more accurate decisions than smaller groups as long as the deliberations of individuals are unbiased and independent— two weighty conditions that honeybees satisfy. First, the colony entertains a wide range of options obtained by information-gathering scouts. That is, they remove bias by broadly sampling the terrain. Too often, companies using a top-down management style provide a narrow array of alternatives since they are generated by the imaginations of a few. In contrast, the decision about a swarm's new residence isn't dominated by the opinions of a couple of bees. Fellow bees attend to the presentation of any scout with a possible landing site even if the location eventually proves to be of relatively inferior quality.

Second, alternatives are independently scrutinized in order to prevent the propagation of errors. Individual assessors personally visit the sites selected by scouts. Bees don't commit to bad ideas because the assessors are able to evaluate the nominated sites at arm's length (wing's length) from the advocates of those sites. In organizations, however, interdependencies among decision makers can ignite a chain reaction of blind conformity. In deferring to the opinions of those whose views are most influential, committees may at times air too few options and short-circuit exploratory discussion. The unintended outcome is that group members agree to a course of action that objective, outside observers might regard as shortsighted or foolish. There is plenty of evidence from the social sciences indicating that people often interpret events and make decisions based on what others believe and do.

Bees avoid decision-making pitfalls by considering many "opinions" that they disinterestedly evaluate. Organizations can do the same but this involves working through human dispositions that limit openness and impartiality. For example, some leaders believe that they have all of the good ideas and that employees must follow unquestioningly. Companies that confer monopolies on ideas will be left with too few choices that are too thinly assessed. Many corporate disasters can be traced to flawed decision-making processes in which relevant alternatives or decision criteria were overlooked or dismissed in favor of assertive, but unproven, points of view.

In contrast to decisions made in haste and for the wrong reasons, some companies have perfectionist leanings. They engage in exhaustive research and analysis and hesitate to act even when their research seems to have reached its conclusion. This state of affairs is handily tagged as "paralysis by analysis." Despite all the fact-finding, these organizations fail to take action—inertia that bees clearly overcome.

In human organizations, this debilitating inertia can be due to many things, but fear and doubt are at the top of the list: doubt in the veracity of claims being made and in the capabilities of the people to effectively execute, and fear that the decisions made may be wrong. Effective leaders go with what they have, use what is available, and do the best they know how.

More Pollen

Few decisions can be made with certainty, but good decisions can be made. The most pressing problems seldom have ready answers, but that needn't deter you from making decisions and moving forward. The bees are able to perform quite nicely with incomplete information because they reduce the risks of their decisions by squeezing prejudices out of the decision processes. You can do the same.

Make sure you sample a range of possibilities and obtain an independent assessment of the alternatives. A well-run brainstorming session can generate a set of choices. Group methods, such as prediction markets or the Delphi technique, offer objective ways to evaluate the options generated. In fact, the Delphi technique has many similarities to the consensus building of bees. Decision makers independently rate each alternative and briefly state the reasons for their assessments. The results are compiled and shared with members of the group who then individually recast their votes. This process continues until a consensus gradually builds around one of the choices. As information is accumulated and shared, the attitudes of the group members converge on one of several possible solutions, as occurs in the hive.

Another technique to free decisions from bias is to call out instances where discussion is evasive or slanted. John Pepper, the former CEO of Procter & Gamble and now chairman of the board at Disney, once told me that at Procter & Gamble they would say "There is a moose on the table" to publicly convey that important issues were being ignored and discussion was becoming obtuse or evasive. Perhaps you can say "The bees are in the hive" to call out a group analysis where there is a poor sampling of opinion and choices are insufficiently explored.

GOING MY WAY

A Lesson in Message Clarity and Acceptance

The renowned sociobiologist Martin Lindauer was one of the first to hypothesize that fast-moving "streaker" bees directionally focus the movement of swarms. As a swarm becomes airborne, streaker bees show the way by shooting through the loosely woven mass of swarming bees in the direction of their new home. Remarkably, thousands of bees remain loosely clustered in flight despite having the freedom of the open skies to scatter. Crucially, the swarm moves with purpose and without stragglers challenging the decision and separating from the group en route. Invariably, they reach their destination. However, what would happen if a swarm was presented with conflicting information by streaker bees going in two different directions? A group of researchers (Latty, Duncan, and Beekman) put this question to the test. They developed swarms and enticed the bees to fly to an especially attractive nest box located across an open field. Swarms found their way to the nest box without difficulty provided that there was no interference in the communications they received from the streaker bees.

On the other hand, test swarms that were forced to contend with forager bees moving perpendicular across the swarm's flight path at speeds commensurate with streakers were unable to find their way to the nest box. Indeed, only one of the test swarms succeeded. More typically, the swarms split and followed circuitous, errant courses.

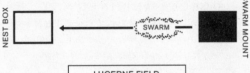

Diagram 1 Mixed Messages

Lucerne is a pasture or forage crop with a blue-violet flower—also known as alfalfa.

BASED ON LATTY, T., DUNCAN, M., AND BEEKMAN, M. (2009). "HIGH BEE TRAFFIC DISRUPTS TRANSFER OF DIRECTIONAL INFORMATION IN FLYING HONEYBEE SWARMS," *ANIMAL BEHAVIOUR* 78, 117–121. REPRINTED BY PERMISSION OF ELSEVIER.

Thus, honeybees provide a natural demonstration of the value of consistent communications for achieving your group's goals. But there is a more subtle point as well. When a swarm lifts off, less than 5 percent of the bees know where they are going—the majority of bees have never visited their future nest. In addition, many bees will never see a streaker bee. What they do notice, however, are the movements of their nearest neighbors. An uninformed bee will move in the direction of the bees around her. As some bees change direction and fly off course, so will others. In this way, conflicting messages can have a compound, disruptive influence on groups beyond the direct effects on the message recipients.

LESSON 7

ORDER AND INNOVATE
THROUGH FUZZY CONSTANTS

During one period of my career, I did a considerable amount of consulting to information technology departments of large companies, mainly concerning organizational design. I learned that creative programmers are not particularly fond of meddlesome programming restrictions, preferring to write freely in elegant lines of code. However, without rigorous and informed standards in place, these programmers' creativity was not used effectively, and the systems they developed did not work very well. In addition, the multiple systems that they built were largely unintegrated and uncommunicative. Instead of spending their days writing the beautiful, efficient code to which they aspired, they spent an inordinate—and frustrating—amount of time modifying each other's work, reprogramming, and patching systems. Newcomers to the department were utterly lost within a tangle of cumbersome and confusing programs.

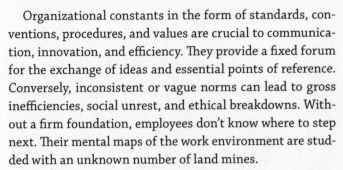

Organizational constants in the form of standards, conventions, procedures, and values are crucial to communication, innovation, and efficiency. They provide a fixed forum for the exchange of ideas and essential points of reference. Conversely, inconsistent or vague norms can lead to gross inefficiencies, social unrest, and ethical breakdowns. Without a firm foundation, employees don't know where to step next. Their mental maps of the work environment are studded with an unknown number of land mines.

Much of the activity of bees is calibrated to constants that allow them to find their way to and from home. During flight, images move across the retinas of their eyes, creating a sense of "optic flow." They adjust their movements and speed to the velocity of this flow. As objects get closer, flow accelerates and the bee slows down. As objects move farther away, flow slows down and the bee speeds up. The bees' "flowometer" allows them to regulate their velocities and flight paths according to different visual cues, such as the textures and proximity of objects, as well as to forces, such as wind speed.

Optic flow is important in part because it provides a common mode of communicating distances. It is the measure the honeybees use to tell each other how far they will have to travel to reach a flower patch. They take in data and summarize it as the speed of motion of images in their environment, or as flow. Bees do not carry maps with conversion keys; optic flow operates as an internal pedometer. They communicate these flows in their waggle dances, providing a fixed reference that takes into account such variables as flying conditions, elevations, and terrain.

The clever bee communicates direction in its dance by relying on another standard, the angle between the position of the sun and the site of the flower patch. In performing their dance, the bees reproduce the angle inside the hive using a straight line up through the hive to stand for the direction of the sun and an intersecting line to represent the direction of the flower patch (visualize the angle formed by the hands of a clock, one on 12 and the other, say, on 2). Outside of the hive, the bees then follow this path using the sun as the reference point and the angle previously communicated within the hive: the flower patch is, for example, at two o'clock.

Constants keep the bees from literally losing their way. An organization's ethical foundations keep companies together when things are most likely to fall apart and the tugs of temptation and desperation are greatest. What allows successful leaders to hold fast when stresses exert pressure to let go? How do leaders know what critical moves to make when circumstances are most dire? The existence of standards and practices. Managers who do not think they need to exercise ethical and procedural discipline during times of plenty will be poorly prepared when conditions worsen. Adherence to organizational constants comes naturally in the hive but requires habit formation in our institutions. As President Kennedy once remarked, "The time to repair the roof is when the sun is shining."

When an organization adopts and fastens itself to a few immutable principles, the system as a whole becomes more reliable. A degree of error in the form of initiative, original

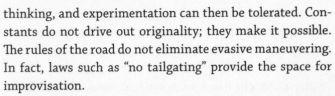

thinking, and experimentation can then be tolerated. Constants do not drive out originality; they make it possible. The rules of the road do not eliminate evasive maneuvering. In fact, laws such as "no tailgating" provide the space for improvisation.

Indeed, honeybees permit a little randomness, or error, to infiltrate their system, sometimes purposely, and sometimes not. When high-quality flower patches are close to the hive or especially large, the directions bees give to one another (through the "round dance") tend to be imprecise, akin to "Go somewhere over there and you'll find something good." This provides a wider distribution of bees over areas that are convenient to scout or are known to be profitable.

Scientists also posit that bees have something like a rule of optimal error. A certain number of bees that are recruited to flower patches get lost en route. Recruits don't always find their way on their first attempts and occasionally these "lost recruits" stumble upon more lucrative flowers. Bees allow an inkling of adaptive inaccuracy because perfect information and an inalterable regimen are important only in static environments where there is one, and only one, profitable food source that persists over an extended period. Where several solutions exist in shifting, complex settings, organizations require the intrusion of some variability—but never to the point of disorder.

Fuzzy constants provide a company with the means to order the workplace and to fence in permissible behaviors without forcing out spontaneity, creativity, and individual judgment. Moreover, fuzzy constants are not "messy." Former secretary of defense Donald Rumsfeld made the word *messy* somewhat fashionable when describing the nature of complex operations such as, in this case, the aftermath of an invasion. It quickly became a convenient description for anything that is hard to predict, control, and organize, insinuating that a measure of disarray is acceptable. Disarray, however, is not acceptable. "Messy" is an index of poor planning and a lack of constants. Although companies exist within wildly competitive and unpredictable markets, the best ones are not messy at all. Their physical environments are neat, their operating protocols, forms, and scripts are consistent, and their value systems are entrenched. They know who they are, what they are doing, and where they are headed.

More Pollen

As I wrote this book, I wondered if any company practices many of the lessons that I lay out. One company comes to mind—Johnson & Johnson. In 1943, before Johnson & Johnson (J&J) became a publicly traded company, Robert Wood Johnson wrote the credo that the company lives by to this day. It sets a standard that guides behavior just as honeybees use standards that are embedded in their dances to point the way. Overall, it defines how the company is expected to relate to various constituencies, including how employees should relate to one another. It contains a set of principles that obviously cannot prescribe every conceivable behavior, but the statements of the credo are not ethically ambiguous either. They clearly articulate a vision of what it means to be a part of the J&J community. Is it harder for the company to conduct its affairs when the credo comes face-to-face with fringe business practices or corporate blunders? Not at all—the existence of constants makes it easier to make the proper choices and to right wrongs. Advertising ethical absolutes is by no means a fail-safe remedy for the moral breaches that have besieged corporate America, but it is superior to allowing a market mentality to regulate behavior purely in terms of costs and benefits. As this book went to press, J&J finds itself in a mess. It has been accused by the FDA of moving too slowly to investigate possible contamination of certain over-the-counter drugs and by the Department of Justice of paying kickbacks to a large pharmacy group. Let's see if the credo helps the company to navigate its ethical way forward.

Even Starbucks has gotten religion lately, concluding that discipline can be a friend to efficiency and creativity. A culture that was once resistant to standards has now embraced them, metaphorically touting their transformation as "celebrating the line": a reference to the new practice of etching lines onto the steaming pitchers for milk so that the baristas can accurately determine the amount needed for each drink—and reduce waste. It used to be that baristas guessed and poured millions of dollars of unused milk down the drain. Starbucks can still ad-lib on drinks, but having baseline recipes for concoctions makes it easier, not harder, to cater to the unique tastes of customers. The "line" provides a predictable experience that can be adjusted as desired.

SAYING WHAT YOU MEAN AND HEARING WHAT WAS MEANT IS HARDER THAN YOU THINK

A car is stopped at a light and the driver yells out to you for directions to the train station as you walk by. The light has turned green, so you haven't much time to convey instructions as the horns of impatient drivers have begun to sound. "Go three lights, turn left, then take your first right, and you'll see the signs for the station." Of course, communications are never that simple. Does the driver count the light he's sitting at as one of the three? In addition, there are two possible rights, one that is perpendicular to the road the driver is traveling and one that emanates from a fork in the road. Which right did you mean?

All communication in the service of balancing meaning and efficiency has elements of imprecision on both the producer and receiver sides. Isn't it extraordinary, then, that an animal a half inch long can travel over a mile to an advertised destination, and, more often than not, find it? Like us, they get it wrong at times. More often than not, however, they get it right. They succeed because they express information in a uniform, structured way that is collectively understandable. If we did the same, we'd take some of the ambiguity out of our communications—just by knowing, for example, that the third light always includes the one you're at.

Karl von Frisch deciphered the dance language of honeybees and was awarded the Nobel Prize in Physiology and Medicine for his painstaking work. He suspected a language in bees since he noticed that once a bee found a flower patch, others would soon follow. Moreover, he deduced that the bees were using the position of the sun as a reference point in their communications. He based this on his observation that bees "danced" in opposite directions depending on whether they visited a particular patch in the morning or in the late afternoon.

The bees' waggle dance is a type of compass that replaces the magnetic field of due north with the position of the sun. The dance gets its name from the shaking that the bees incorporate into their routine. As shown in part (a) of the diagram, the dancer starts out on a line, waggles, then continues forward before moving counterclockwise in a semicircle, returning to the point of origin. She then repeats the process but moves clockwise on the next circuit, continuing in this figure-eight fashion with the number of rotations corresponding to her enthusiasm for her find.

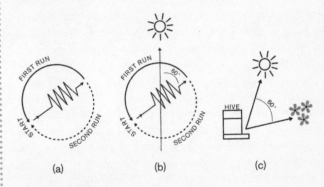

Diagram 2 Communication Standards

What is the bee saying to fellow foragers? Given that straight up on the comb represents the sun, the dancer is saying, "When you exit the hive, the flower patch is sixty degrees to the right of the sun." Part (b) of the diagram shows the dance inside the hive and part (c) illustrates what happens when the bee exits the hive. The length of the waggle phase of the dance is directly correlated with the distance to the flower patch. The waggle is a translation of optic flow.

All together, then, the dance succinctly conveys "how far," "how good," and "which way."

LESSON 8

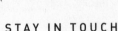

STAY IN TOUCH

Nothing may be more essential to the survival of the hive than ongoing feedback. Without doubt, it is a necessary condition of survival. How else can organisms react to changes occurring around them unless they have the means to remain intimately connected to their environs?

However, organizations sometimes lose touch with their customers and competition, and this isolation from reality is a recurrent source of corporate failure. Any company that experiences a protracted decline in market share without taking corrective action is in some way suffering from a faulty feedback system. Something gets lost in translation from the generation of information to the production of a response. A. G. Lafley, the former CEO of Procter & Gamble, once remarked that one of the CEO's most central tasks is maintaining an intimate connection between the external world and the internal organization.

Bees manage to keep their activities closely coupled with

external conditions. Most notably, they have a simple feed-back system tied to the quality and amounts of nectar they gather in a highly volatile environment. Foragers return to the hive with nectar. Receiver bees back at the hive await the foragers' arrival in order to off-load the nectar and store it away in the comb as honey. The hive is like a very busy distribution center: trucks (foragers) pull up to the docks where the goods are unloaded and stowed by workers (receivers) on warehouse shelves.

Now suppose that a trucker pulls into the center and cannot find a bay to discharge his goods. What happens then? If you have ever seen a distribution center, you know what happens. The trucks form a queue and wait for a slot to open. The truckers are responding to a simple feedback loop. The saturation of bays at the warehouse informs drivers that there is a delay and to take their place in waiting based on a set rule such as first come, first served. Truckers continue to monitor the situation and adjust their behavior according to developments within the warehouse.

This practice seems reasonable to us, but it doesn't work this way in the hive. This would be like receiver bees turning away foragers who are bringing in the precious nectar. Perhaps this is why the foragers, who know more about the outside world, control the conversation, and not the inwardly focused receivers. Making foragers arbitrarily wait before they can deliver their goods would be like turning away customers.

Regrettably, it is possible for businesses to turn customers away. It seems hard to believe—why would you refuse money from someone who is trying to give it to you? Often, the problem arises when the company begins to focus on internal metrics that take precedence over the demands of the marketplace. Suddenly the customer doesn't matter as much.

A disconnect between the outside and inside world may occur, for example, when cost-cutting measures come at the price of neglecting legitimate customer needs. Companies that take quality out of products by replacing good components with cheaper ones, that understaff or replace knowledgeable sales personnel with less expensive, inexperienced personnel, or that install a severe, no-returns policy may be pushing customers out the door through inferior goods, longer lines, limited expertise, or inconvenience.

When returning foragers take an extended amount of time to locate a receiver bee with whom to exchange nectar, foragers perform a tremble dance and emit a piping sound. These communications indicate that the hive has more nectar than it can handle, and that more receivers are required as well as fewer foragers. The honeybees are managing the measure of the time it takes to exchange nectar or, as the experts say, the "latency" of exchange. Simply adding receivers wouldn't restore the desired exchange rate quickly enough, so the bees send out a "stop" signal to fellow foragers as well, telling them that no more foragers are required. The foragers realize, then, that they have to do something with the overflow of "trucks" by regulating how many come in at any given time. The bees are not oblivious to their organizational limits. While they make an effort to use as much of their available resources as possible, they also know that it is not realistic to expand operations to accommodate any number of foragers when their hive faces genuine constraints. Though honeybees have a natural bias in favor of consumption, they nevertheless try not to take on more than they can handle.

Honeybees use what I consider the Holy Grail of feedback. Their feedback contains the wonderful feature of directly uniting external conditions and the state of the colony to their activity. That is, the colony is constantly monitoring how it is performing and what it must do to improve. A long latency between a forager's return and handoff of nectar conveys that it is very nice outside and that the nectar inflow currently is more than the colony can manage. A very short latency indicates that times are tough and the colony requires a greater influx of nectar. In the latter case, honeybees use the waggle dance to redeploy workers as foragers, as well as to communicate the direction and distance of food sources. The bees also may use shaking signals to arouse quiescent foragers and direct them to the dance floor, where they, in turn, can follow the lead of waggle dancers to select flower patches. The colony, then, constantly adjusts its operations to circumstances to ensure the most efficient nectar intake.

It isn't easy for companies to conjure such elegance in measurement and feedback, but it can be done. Cisco Systems, the networking corporation, has implemented a system that enables the company to track worldwide orders from sales teams daily, and to evaluate and quickly react to trends within regions and market segments. Cisco also uses its high-tech facilities to relay information and instructions among staff at its corporate offices and the fifty-thousand-plus people in the field. At the end of the month, Cisco knows how well it performed within four hours of closing its books.

More Pollen

The honeybee is adept at using measurement and feedback to stay in touch with its floral environment and the current state of the hive. Bees are constantly taking in data that specifically and immediately inform them what it's like outside the hive. What's more, based on that information honeybees know how to react. Feedback is most helpful when it conveys what you can do, starting now, to become more successful in your field of activity. The more directive the information, the better the feedback is.

More precisely, you know feedback is good if it enables you to consider four possible adaptive options: 1) whether you should change the way you do things to accommodate the demands of the world outside (e.g., add services); 2) whether you should change the external environment in some manner to better suit your interests and capabilities (e.g., teach customers how to use your technologies more often and effectively); 3) whether you should try to exclude others from your competitive field by changing the rules (e.g., lobby regulators for licensing requirements for new service providers); 4) and whether you should get out while you still can (e.g., abandon the product or service). Finally, of course, you can always do nothing if the feedback suggests you are on the right track.

The closer a measurement is to behaviors you can

implement to produce a desired outcome, the more useful is the feedback obtained with that measurement. Here is a simple example. Let's say I want to lose weight and therefore weigh myself every morning. But as it happens, I never shed a pound. In fact, I gain weight. How can that be? Well, how much I weigh doesn't tell me anything about what I should do. However, if I counted calories ingested and burned and examined their effect on my weight, I would know whether further changes were necessary.

Outcome measures such as weight and revenues are generally insufficient by themselves because they are too distant from adaptive behaviors to be effective. The management guru Henry Mintzberg satirically refers to the vacuum between operational necessity and management edict as "deeming." This is the simpleton method of management that, for example, mandates a certain percentage increase in sales without ever considering and monitoring the particular actions needed for success.

LESSON 9

KEEP IT SIMPLE

Often organizations introduce a level of complexity into their processes and products that inadvertently undermines efficiency and effectiveness. That is, over time, corporate operations and goods become Rube Goldberg creations. Rube Goldberg was an American cartoonist best known for his drawings of complicated machines that performed simple tasks. Today we honor him through the many engineering contests held in his name. Individuals or teams receive awards for building the most convoluted contraptions to achieve simple outcomes such as turning on a light or breaking an egg. Although we might not all win a Rube Goldberg prize, we unnecessarily complicate our work in many ways. I briefly describe three of the major ones here, but keep in mind that this by no means exhausts the possibilities.

One common way that we overengineer goods and services is by feeling compelled to incorporate the ideas of every conceivable constituency into the final design. The many quips about committees (for example, the unwilling picked from the unfit to do the unnecessary) are nods to the ineffective solutions that many hours of group discussion can produce.

A second way to do ourselves in is by building on existing platforms that have inherent limitations, making it hard to do what you want. For example, as I write, there are electricians at our house, good people and true professionals. Some time ago, we had a couple of small lights installed in our front yard (by a different crew) and now we were looking to add more lights. The crew chief explained to me that the system they use is not entirely compatible with our existing system. That means that the electricians would have to run wires here and there, connect timers at this place and that, and fuss around in our fuse box to get everything working in harmony. Ultimately, we decided to replace the old system rather than build on top of it and wind up with something that might not function properly. We ate our original costs and spent a little more for the new system, but we will not have to pay for the endless workarounds and inevitable fixes, and we will have a system that runs smoothly.

Finally, we sometimes try to design for the exceptions. Rather than create a product or process for the 99 percent of the people who are good, law-abiding citizens, we incorporate features that try to exclude or capture the 1 percent of users (abusers) who will attempt to circumvent our intent. I recently read about a product that fits nicely with this approach. The State Liquor Control Board of Pennsylvania is thinking about installing wine kiosks at select sites. Of course, we would not want the intoxicated or underaged buying alcohol, so purchasers will have to insert their driver's licenses and breathe into a Breathalyzer to complete the transaction. The intentions are good, but the result is that you irritate the people whom you want as customers while providing teens with an easy challenge.

When it comes to the hive, honeybees keep it simple. They get right to the point, concisely, clearly, and without undue complication. There are several aspects of what they do from which we could learn. These will not overcome all potential barriers to simplicity, but keeping the following three maxims in mind will help.

First, the information exchange among bees is *relevant*. This way, when a bee receives a signal, it knows it means something important. They do not communicate any more or less than is necessary. For instance, there is no feedback signal in the hive that tells bees to abandon a poor flower patch. That information does not help anyone. Bees working the same patch already know the quality there is poor and the information is not pertinent to foragers who work at other patches. In addition, bees recruit unemployed foragers to good patches—it would not make sense to tell them about all the places not to go.

Second, bees have clear standards that regulate their behavior. The standards keep their mission on track and protect against wrongheaded commitments. When foragers return to the hive, they express their enthusiasm for the quality (e.g., sugar concentration) of the nectar they have found through their waggle dances. As you might imagine, if all the bees had a different idea of what constitutes a "good" flower patch, then the colony could mobilize to the wrong places. An excited bee returns to the hive and recruits others to the site, some of whom then return to recruit more bees, and so on. Thus it would take only an errant few to get the hive started in the wrong direction. I have seen eager and enthusiastic authorities in companies mobilize people and resources around new businesses that made absolutely no sense and, in retrospect, would have been difficult to justify had the definition of desirable "patches" of business "nectar" been clearly established from the start. The integrity of communication is possible because the entire foraging force has common criteria and understanding about the true value of one of its chief products.

Third, there is elegance and parsimony to what honeybees do. At times, this involves dodging solutions that seem the most logical but may not be. Honeybees, for example, do not "cross-train" foragers and receivers so that one may take the place of the other. That is, they do not use task switching to try to balance work capacities, minimize queuing delays, and maximize the import of nectar. Instead, they elect to pull from a reserve workforce of foragers. For honeybees, bringing in more workers to exploit a ripe situation is more important than keeping a fixed resource such as the proportion of foragers to receivers perfectly balanced. It is safe to say that where trade-offs exist in the hive, the colony will favor the equivalent of revenue intake over nifty accounting and administrative rigor.

Additionally, there are two efficiency-related reasons why switching between tasks is not a very good option in this case. First, foraging takes time to perfect (there is a learning curve) and the "cross-trained" receivers would not be as good at it. Second, receivers would not be able to assume the role of forager until they had completed their current job of transferring the nectar into the comb for storage as honey, thereby introducing a costly time delay.

Hypothetically, here is what might occur if the hive behaved like some companies. The "company" hive assumes that the problem of too few foragers (or too many receivers) must be corrected based on the bees that are currently involved in the exchange of nectar. As a solution, they adopt task switching between the groups as the solution. For companies, this solution has the perceived advantage of cost neutrality since the adjustments involve the periodic re-arrangement of a fixed resource pool. Thus, implicit in this decision is the use of cost containment as the governing standard. Soon, however, the company notices that it needs to supplement the receiver corps, because the receivers are taking too long to off-load their nectar before they are redeployed. Therefore, the company introduces temporary receivers to supplement the receivers—thereby adding new features to an existing process platform. The company also institutes training sessions for receivers and occasionally pulls them off-line for remedial instruction on the fine art of foraging. After some time has passed, and as experience with the system grows, people begin to think, "There has to be a better way."

Although this is a hypothetical example in which I have given the bees human qualities, I do know that we sometimes have a tendency to make things more difficult than they need to be. We can save ourselves a lot of trouble if we keep our feedback on point, our standards clear, and our solutions as simple as possible.

More Pollen

The best plans often are the simplest, involving clear, direct, and uncomplicated communications and actions. Colonies execute with as little waste in resources, communications, and personal energy as possible. Granted, they have had a long time to work things out, but their wondrously successful society remains brilliantly straightforward.

Simplicity is a consequence of knowing what you are talking about, doing, and want. In part, achieving clarity of perspective and direction depends on the use of a common method of analysis to examine problems. A standard approach provides organizational members with a mutual vocabulary and framework for defining concepts, proposing relationships, conducting tests, assessing consequences, determining goals, and, in turn, putting the proper mechanisms in place (e.g., feedback, tracking).

A useful simplicity also depends on recognizing when enough is enough. When Jeff Kindler took over as CEO of Pfizer, he and his staff pared the corporate focus to one objective: boosting the number of compounds that get to market. Then they set about to streamline the drug development process by removing organizational layers and the number of internal review committees, reducing the geographic expanse of research facilities, and quickly killing off products without promise. Kindler's revelation as he took over at Pfizer was that the entire corporate apparatus had become too complex, cumbersome, and slow. Perhaps the wise, successful businessman Henry David Thoreau (many pundits would say he was a much better pencil-maker than writer) was right: "Our life is frittered away by detail . . . simplify, simplify."

LESSON 10

FIND YOUR ZEITGEBERS

A scattered team of commandos prepares for their assault on a munitions plant behind enemy lines. It is late at night. Team members expectantly glance at their watches and, at just the right moment, begin their advance, converging on the plant in unison. They quietly and methodically set the facility ablaze and, as the deadly flames are about to engulf them, they are lifted to safety thanks to the timely arrival of helicopters. Whew!

This bit of bad fiction glosses over the real complexity of the mission. The success of the mission here depended on several factors: opportune timing of the operation, a method to coordinate the actions of members, and a way to keep all mission personnel and project teams on high alert and in a state of readiness.

To briefly illustrate how these operational basics can easily run afoul, consider a simple chore such as a trip to the supermarket that, in our family, we have a habit of getting wrong. Somehow, my wife and I always manage to go at the most congested time, I lose my spouse (whose cell phone is dead—again) in the store, and we are forsaken by children who promised to help unload and stock groceries but are nowhere to be found when we need them (because we "took too long to get home"). Exponentially increase the difficulty of the task and the number of people involved, and you have an organization filled with supersize problems of execution.

Honeybees organize around their primary mission, which in the service of survival and reproduction is the retrieval of nectar and pollen. The peak harvesttime for each varies by the time of day and type of flower, and, therefore, the bees establish a tempo that coincides with the periods in which nectar and pollen are at their highest levels. As with the commandos, some times are better for action than others.

Honeybees have daily rhythms that connect their activity to the environment in ways that yield functional advantages. They anticipate times (and places) in which they are most likely to find success, and mobilize during those periods. In essence, they establish routines that are synchronized to the times that will give them the highest returns for their invested energies. Such a time cue is known as a "zeitgeber" (pronounced "tsahyt-gey-ber" from the German for "time-giver"). Although these daily rhythms may have biological bases, the zeitgebers of bees develop over time and can be extinguished, suggesting there is a learned component involved.

The idea of a zeitgeber is to establish a relationship with one's environment in ways that make an organization or individual more responsive to what is happening in the environment. Rhythms are all around us. Your daily commute and lunch break are timed events. If you schedule them well, your day goes more smoothly. A company that ramps up for the holiday season or a person who hops into bed nightly at ten is acting according to times that signal periods of greater intensity or periods of rest.

The bees establish a beat that makes sense to them. The everyday routines of the hive are convenient ways to productively organize the collective and direct its actions. Their common clock and schedule is a low-tech form of automation that removes excessive costs of planning from the equation. Zeitgebers are helpful in instituting order, control, and calm in what would otherwise be the chaotic interplay between creature and environment. Managers can achieve much the same results by instituting daily routines and by introducing a sensible regularity to meetings, briefings, and such, or, on a grander scale, by calibrating corporate-wide activities to seasonal events, typical product cycles, or the anticipated actions of competitors.

Routines aligned with the natural rhythms of a habitat (whether the outdoors or the marketplace) are an excellent start to operational efficiency, but a general organizational tempo is not enough to ensure precise coordination in a dynamic environment. The commandos cannot begin their approach at roughly the same time and bees cannot forage at an approximate hour. In circumstances in which every second counts in the hive, honeybees have refined ways to harmonize work through various forms of communication.

One method bees use to coordinate their activities is very twentieth century. They communicate with one another, face-to-face, or antennae to antennae. In a dark cavern, much of what bees have to say to one another actually gets across through tactile exchanges. In the spirit of preventing a nightmare scenario for Human Resources, I am not specifically advocating this form of communication. However, organizations can inspire meaningful exchanges through the judicious use of meetings and spaces that promote spontaneous encounters. In the age of the microchip, electronics still cannot totally replace the personal.

Honeybees also have a remarkably sophisticated knowledge management system by which information is reliably stored and dispersed. The communication center for foraging activities is the dance floor of the colony. This is where bees go to catch up on the latest news and to learn how and where they are needed. Unlike many information centers, whether bulletin boards or servers, the dance floor of honeybees is continuously updated. In fact, if you sit and watch bees come and go from the hive, they resemble the constant flow of golden data packets on an invisible optic thread.

The information center of the hive is a parallel and distributed operating system. It is parallel in that the range of data inputs (i.e., the number of contributing bees) is extremely wide and the bees carry redundant information. If one packet of information is lost in transmission, it will be replaced by another. Redundancy principally exists when the information provided is critical. For example, more bees will advertise the best flower patches, so the most repetitious data occur when excellent foraging opportunities exist and honeybees can little afford to lose sight of them. Therefore, the honeybees' communication system is able to provide reliable data even if some of the information goes missing or is misconstrued.

"Distributed" means that the information that reaches the dance floor comes straight from the field and is uncontaminated by the data massaging of intermediaries who may have a vested interest in how the information is interpreted. The data is not filtered through organizational layers, as often happens in hierarchies. Instead, the information center of honeybees is a lot like YouTube or Wikipedia, where individuals can freely present whatever they "find." It is a sweeping interactive reservoir of searchable data points. And, like Wikipedia, the information contained on the dance floor is self-correcting in that inferior information (i.e., poorer places to harvest) doesn't last as long as superior information. In the hive, good data is always overwhelming the bad.

Knowledge management systems, even those that are of the highest quality, require a lot of initiative to use. In companies, information frequently sits as an inert glob. The information is there but people forget about it or are too busy to do anything with it. In the hive, fellow bees are directed to places where important information resides through an intranet by which they tap out low-frequency signals to one another. The tips around the hexagonal wax cells are slightly elevated and form an excellent conductor for vibrating code. Where the bees are densely packed, the signals are blocked, but where the bees are loosely configured and spaced farther apart, the signals travel farther. This functions as an internal RSS (Really Simplified Syndication) feed that informs bees standing on the periphery of where it's all happening and that there is something interesting they should come and see. Gaps in the bees' knowledge, then, are quickly filled by sending out notifications.

Regardless of the specific information communicated to one another, the bees throughout the hive know when they are on "high alert" and a phase of increased activity is under way. This state of preparedness commences with the up-tempo of harvesttime. As the activity of the hive increases in time to match external conditions, the outer regions of the hive heat up. The thermal cues, then, serve as a colony-wide clock that tells the bees throughout the hive to energize.

Back to our zeitgebers: creating daily habits and rituals that intimately connect to the organization's primary foci is a way to get the blood flowing and to stir activity, which then feeds off itself. Energy can be self-perpetuating, as in the hive. The rhythms awaken the bees to increased activity, which heats the hive, which sustains higher levels of activity, and so on. The best way to get active is to start moving. Zeitgebers can help.

More Pollen

Colonies have organizational rhythms that are attuned to opportunities in the ever-changing flower market. These rhythms are further refined by communication and an accurate knowledge management system, thereby enabling colony members to coordinate their activities. There is a logical flow to this: rhythms + coordination = efficiency.

When routines are fixed for groups of people, as when

business hours begin and end at a certain time, it becomes easier to coordinate workers' activities. Establishing daily patterns is like having an invisible coxswain who paces and synchronizes the actions of a rowing team. Attending as she does to other boats on the water during a competitive race, the coxswain's guidance is sensitive to the events transpiring around her, while ongoing communication unifies the team's actions. The vitality of the team is made possible with rhythmic activity that is coordinated by timely communications, as well as an updated pool of data that tells the team precisely where it stands. To keep a department, division, or company alive, it helps to have a pulse.

Let's briefly look at an example to illustrate the intuitiveness and benefits of routines. As a leader, you meet every Tuesday with your department managers individually at a specified time. Tuesdays make the most sense because sales figures are refreshed and customer inquiries are tabulated the prior evening. The schedule enables everyone to exchange and act on information according to the established beat. Once together, it is easier to evaluate the status of the department and plan what needs to be done.

Closer to home—literally—imagine the difference between a household that operates to a beat (e.g., wake times, dinner, preparation for bed, and such) and one whose style, shall we say, is more free-form. Which family does more together, is more efficient at tending to household chores, and is less stressed?

LESSON 11

DESIGN "FLEXIGID" SYSTEMS

Division of labor was practiced within the animal kingdom many millions of years before manufacturers of the new industrial age began producing widgets for the masses. As manufacturing grew in complexity, more people became specialized operators and more parts became standardized as ways to accelerate production times and minimize costly, time-consuming process variations. Today we accept division of labor, or specialization in task performance, as an organizational staple. However, it suffers from one big problem: complete, or strict, division of labor is an inflexible form of organization. Division of labor is extremely beneficial in constant environments but can be maladaptive in changing ones.

Honeybees have developed a pliable division of labor, a fixed structure that is modifiable according to circumstances. The biological machinery of the hive may be described as "flexigid": at once flexible and rigid, malleable and taut. Honeybees have two types of division of labor: temporal and functional. Temporal specialization refers to bees that develop over time according to maturity and experience. Bees progress from serving inside the honeycombed walls of the hive to the world outside. Eventually, the top bees become foragers, demonstrating a form of specialization in which maturing abilities are matched to more challenging and risky tasks. Moreover, foragers increase in proficiency the longer they have been in the field. In essence, bees forage at different levels of sophistication, ranging from entry to advanced levels. What's more, a "senior forager" in the hive really is better at foraging than a "junior forager," and the colony depends on that tangible improvement for the efficacy of the entire hive.

Progressions in organizations are supposed to work in this manner with time-based steps denoting real differences in specialization and abilities. In many respects, whether honeybee colony or human institution, the better the match between job requirements and individuals' abilities, the more efficient the organization.

In honeybee colonies, functional specialization refers to the physiological attributes of bees that enable or limit what they can do. For example, drones physically cannot carry nectar even if they wanted to. Certain jobs in the hive can be done only by bees that are physically equipped to do them. This type of specialization, then, is a result of unique functional abilities that give groups of bees such as nurses and foragers distinction—a little like organizational departments where employees contain relatively homogeneous skill sets. Again, it is easy to see that certain work is most efficiently performed by those—the experts—with select abilities to effectively carry it out.

All of us have firsthand experience with specialized parts that fail because they are defective, overloaded, or dead. These parts can be spark plugs, microchips, heart valves, or marketers, and their failure can result in sputtering performance or a thunderous crash. Similarly, a company's direct mail campaign may be postponed while Denise is out sick, or a client may be put on hold in perpetuity while Richard, the dedicated account executive, converses with another caller. But bees can't wait to feed the young or gather more nectar if the need is present. Consequently, bees have evolved several ways to compensate for the temporary loss of specialization so that they can continue to operate productively.

Honeybees have instituted three mechanisms to avoid the calamity of executional breakdown. The first is prevention through prediction. Not even honeybees can afford massive losses in their specialized workforce. Because many foragers can die in rain- and windstorms, they have acquired an ability to forecast and avoid oncoming storms like an army of kids on bikes, racing the thunderclouds for the shelter of home.

Second, bees have what I refer to in my consulting work as embedded staffing plans. These are embedded in the overall strategy of the organization and are a fundamental part of the planning process. Honeybees know how much of which type of labor is required to supply the colony with the resources required to thrive. Of the total members of the hive, a certain number will be functionally divided as nurses, comb builders, foragers, and such. These numbers are subject to modest changes according to conditions, but within a certain degree honeybees know what they are doing.

In contrast, staffing in companies can wildly miss the mark. Staffing "plans" tend to consist of an annual reappraisal of the cost of people, leaving a sizable disconnect between what the company hopes to achieve, what kinds of old and new work will have to be performed, and how many of what kind of people will be needed to execute the work properly. Figuring this out is a challenging, time-consuming, and thought-provoking endeavor, but an exercise that must be done in order for the company to determine if the right people, configured in the right way, are doing the right work.

Third, colonies are able to adjust their workforces. One way they incorporate flexibility is by maintaining a limited number of precocious reserves. You might think of these reserves as "fast-trackers" or "hi-pos" (high-potentials). These bees can develop at a faster rate than ordinary if the colony needs to fill higher-order roles quickly. They also use slack resources or workforce buffers. "As busy as a bee" isn't really an accurate reflection of bees' true activity levels. In fact, 20 to 30 percent of the hive is relatively idle much of the time. For example, not all foragers are foraging at any one time. Some are deployed on other tasks while others simply station themselves in the hive until their services are needed. As some beekeepers have astutely noticed, unoccupied bees can sometimes be seen rocking back and forth at the hive entrance during slow periods like bored teenagers waiting for something to do (the gentle rocking motion of these bees is called "washboarding," named after the seesaw movements of a person scrubbing clothes on a washboard).

In addition, many bees are able to switch between tasks, pitching in when needed. They act as generalists. Whereas not all bees can forage, all foragers can do other things. Thus, colonies have a healthy number of bees that are, in essence, able to work on a number of different tasks. This helps them to make transitions in worker deployments in boom-or-bust economies. Companies similarly demonstrate workforce flexibility when, for example, they reduce the factory times of employees and reassign them to maintenance tasks or enroll them in training sessions during down periods, as steelmaker Nucor recently did. Professional firms such as law firms, accounting houses, and consultancies redeploy people when feasible from declining businesses such as acquisitions to more profitable lines such as corporate restructurings and bankruptcies.

No job is beneath the honeybee when it comes to the survival of the hive. When the hive has urgent needs such as nursing brood, the most distinguished members of the colony, the foragers, will pitch in. They have not lost the physiological aptitude or the experience to serve as a nurse, a job that they recently held. Extrapolating from this example, one effective means of retaining flexibility is to have managers who are willing to roll up their sleeves and help the team when needed.

More Pollen

Organizational responsiveness is best fulfilled by staffing plans and deployments that can be stretched and adapted as conditions warrant. In this regard, honeybees have proven to be masters at contingency planning. Honeybees have figured out that it is imprudent to design structures and processes on the assumption of ideal conditions. Instead, they operate according to the sixteenth-century English proverb "Hope for the best, prepare for the worst." There are many other proverbs of a similar tenor, suggesting that folklore may be on to something. In your own work, it would be wise to ask yourself, "What's the worst that can happen?" before finalizing significant actions. Assuming that a system is impervious to failure can be problematic. If you believe the *Titanic* cannot sink, you may consider every additional lifeboat an extravagance.

A lot can go wrong in business: customers' purchases rise and fall, assembly lines break down, investments go bad, and people use new technologies in inexplicable ways. Honeybees compensate for swings in their fortune by having slack resources, for example, at a real cost to them—but having relatively inactive bees around is worth it. Building contingencies into processes and designs increases costs. However, what is the cost of assuming idyllic circumstances and implementing inelastic structures and systems, then meeting that day when everything goes wrong?

Scenario planning is an essential part of a manager's job. The company pays you the big bucks because one of your primary duties is to anticipate disasters and devise alternatives should they arise. A little bit of forethought can go a long way. No miracle powers are required. In fact, futurist Peter Schwartz has developed a five-step prognostic that is sensible and easy to implement. Briefly, his method involves listing key environmental uncertainties and combining the most significant of these in different ways. For example, suppose the pace of technology and the number of competitors in your market space are the unknowns that you identify as important for the future prospects of your business. Schwartz suggests writing concrete scenarios—as newspaper headlines and clippings—using the interactions of these variables as the foundation. You might consider one plausible future in which the pace of technology quickens and new competitors flock into your market. Once you consider this possible world, you will be in a better position to think about the implications and take precautionary measures.

LESSON 12

PRESERVE A POSITIVE WORKPLACE

Division of labor plays another important role in the life of the hive in addition to the one it plays in the allocation of work. It limits the amount of physical contact that bees performing one type of task have with bees performing other unrelated tasks. Why is that important? It is a way to contain the spread of infestation and disease that can be colony killers.

In the hive, containment includes close control over pathogen transfer points. For example, pollen foragers take their loads directly to the comb without touching any intermediaries that could compromise the quality of the pollen and pass along harmful contaminants to the life-giving source of the hive—the brood.

Bees control epidemics in three other ways, each of which, as you might surmise, has a corollary in our own institutions. First, bees detect, uncap, and discard infected brood so they have no chance of adversely affecting the colony. Thus young bees who clearly have no promising future in the hive and whose continuing presence would grossly interfere with the quality of the colony are swiftly removed.

Second, if a bee is in trouble, it asks for help. It performs a dance that elicits grooming behavior from other bees in order to remove dust, ectoparasites, and so forth. Rather than suffer, honeybees call on others to cleanse them. Bees have no difficulty in requesting assistance when afflicted; nor do they have difficulty in giving it when asked.

Third, although most bees die outside of the hive as foragers, some bees die inside the hive as well. Most sick and infected bees have the good sense to drag themselves from the hive before they become a nuisance to the colony—would that caustic and negative employees do the same. Nevertheless, not all of them make it out. These dead are removed by a small subset of bees appropriately named "undertakers," who carry the carcasses away from the hive. The colony can't afford to have idle bodies lying about. They take up space and the rotting corpses create buggy, noxious cesspools. There really is no other choice for the colony than to rid itself of those who literally have come to the end of their productive lives.

Bees maintain a clean hive and try to ensure that only healthy bees associate with other healthy bees. In order to keep their space pure, they try to curb the transfer of diseases that would interfere with their work and endanger the colony. Remaining true to their evolutionary heritage that the colony's functioning depends upon a positive disease-free environment, the honeybee controls unwanted elements that afflict group performance not only as a means of keeping the bad out, but assuring that the good, in its many manifestations such as health and energy, stays in.

I have been in more than a few companies infested with highly contagious negativity and cynicism. It certainly is easier to manage and rectify attitudinal troubles if they remain isolated. I have found it helpful to think of culture as consisting of a number of pockets of various depths and diameters that ensnare behavior as a sinkhole consumes cars. The wider and deeper the hole, the more pervasive its influence and the harder it becomes to climb out. While I suppose laughter can be contagious, most of the things that tend to spread uncontrolled, like fire, are not good and necessitate mechanisms of confinement. Division of labor is a natural means by which the size of holes is partly restricted.

More Pollen

Bees establish a healthy milieu by maintaining a disease-free hive. They instinctively know that they need to fear not only external threats but also the decay that can occur from within.

Internal rot within a company manifests as cynicism. Cynicism spreads and settles when a company's leadership envisions strategies it has little ability to implement or conjures new initiatives monthly without ever finishing anything it starts. Employees soon realize that every undertaking is doomed, and they either "slow-walk" solutions (i.e., go through the motions) or they easily give up at the first sign of difficulty. The collective thought that nothing is possible is the worst of all possible worlds. Thus, do not give an order for a new effort unless you mean it and are prepared to see it through.

Conversely, the idea of "staying positive" has many connotations in organizations with "satisfaction" as the most common. However, when it comes to productivity, satisfaction is not a particularly strong predictor. Indeed, much of the scientific research suggests that it is overrated. Besides, managers and employees sometimes confuse "staying positive" with incessantly happy messages, unqualified praise, and automatic pay hikes. Rather, the most important frame of mind is for employees to be optimistic about the future and convinced that they can alter it for the better. These follow from the maintenance of a healthy corporate climate in which managers help their employees to be successful.

LESSON 13

KEEP YOUR BALANCE

The activity of a colony appears chaotic to a casual observer. Bees crawl over one another and fly to and from the hive at irregular intervals and in multiple directions. Yet amid this apparent confusion, there is an underlying order. Bees are like kindergartners on May Day. Though the Maypole dance may look a bit messy, the steps have all been choreographed. Tethered to a pole by ribbons, the children have limits to where they can wander. The behavior around the pole is somewhat fluid and occasionally spontaneous, but it is also anchored to facilitate and constrain particular kinds of movements. It doesn't eliminate a child's penchant to ad-lib, but the pole keeps the action tighter and easier to manage. Bees have, and organizations need, the equivalent of the Maypole by which collective action is regulated and stabilized: the antidote to scattered or wayward behavior.

One of the principal ways that bees moderate extreme behaviors is through genetic diversity. Bees introduce diversity into the hive by creating multiple patrilines in which workers have the same queen mother but different fathers. This genetic variability produces bees within the same hive that are differentially sensitive to environmental conditions. For example, bees keep the temperature of the hive relatively constant at about ninety-three degrees Fahrenheit. This is remarkable when you consider the wide fluctuations in temperatures outside the hive. The bees heat the hive by contracting two sets of flight muscles and cool the hive by flapping their wings. However, they don't all act at the same time. If they did, the temperature would alternate between hot and cold at levels far too wide for the bees to tolerate. Fortunately, the bees differ in their sensitivity to temperature and alter their behavior at different times in response to climatic conditions. The result is that the temperature inside the hive remains relatively stable.

Similarly, imagine a passenger ship at sea with all hands on deck. Suppose that everyone on board is identical. Suddenly the ship begins to pitch in one direction. The passengers all respond in like fashion at the same time and run to the opposite side of the ship to correct the tilt. Their collective weight, of course, generates a tilt in the opposite direction, and they rush to the other side in unison to make another adjustment. This pattern continues, with the swings getting steeper and steeper, until the boat capsizes. These oscillations are precisely what the bees are trying to avoid. They do so by having a diverse set of passengers, only some of whom respond as the ship begins to lean. In essence, only some bees go to one side of the ship, or flap their wings, to modify the temperature of the hive, depending on conditions. This won't stop the ship from rocking or the hive from heating or cooling, but it narrows the angle of tilt, or the range of temperatures.

These examples illustrate that the real value of diversity is its tendency to promote organizational stability. Diversity in organizations typically is identified with particular mixes of race and gender designed to observe government regulations and satisfy companies' sense of fairness. Without doubt, workplaces should be nondiscriminatory. However, employee composition in itself ensures diversity only in its most elementary form. Achieving diversity entails much more than a checklist of surface characteristics. Effective hiring also requires attention to the interests, preferences, and talents that make people unique. For example, the Danish enzyme maker Novozymes specifically looks for entrepreneurs in order to benefit from their distinctive outlooks and penchant to add a little grit to the organization to produce pearls. This type of diversity balances organizational discourse and activity and keeps the institution safe. The resultant steadiness may not seem very exciting, but the equilibrium of a well-managed company is far superior to the terrifying experience of swimming for one's life.

Organizations that lack diversity are like the hapless passengers on our capsized ship. They suffer from a concentration of similar strengths and points of view, tilting prevailing thought perilously in one direction. It may be that the company hired too many like-minded people. Or it may be that the company hired well but failed to employ the assorted strengths of their workforce effectively. Despite employees' potential to contribute different insights and ideas on issues, the company's management blocks expression. In doing so, managers negate one of their chief assets, their workforce, by encouraging—or insisting upon—conformity. Rather than have the diverse and able passengers use their brains independently to right the ship, a centralized, hierarchically positioned authority directs them en masse to one side of the ship or the other.

Or, equally unproductive, the manager micromanages individuals in a slow, monotonous fashion by specifying in exhaustive detail every legitimate move an employee can make. Awaiting orders, the passengers do nothing until told to move, creating a different kind of problem. In contrast to the ship that overacts in one direction, micromanagement promotes the type of ships that are indifferent and sluggish to circumstances. Micromanaged organizations end up being controlled by, as opposed to controlling, their environments. In the end, the fate of a ship without balance is the same no matter the particular cause.

More Pollen

Managers should strive to hire capable people who, as a group, provide the team with a range of perspectives and worldviews. Otherwise, organizations can become closed societies. In addition to making a conscious effort to hire in a fair-minded way, take the time to select people who are naturally inquisitive and who have varied interests. Candidates should be evaluated on their hard skills (e.g., accounting), to be sure, yet don't neglect the softer, job-related human factors that can inject vitality into the workplace and profoundly affect performance. If there is any question in your mind about the importance of these soft skills, try a simple thought experiment. Think about the best employees you have ever seen and ask what personal attributes distinguished them from others. I am almost certain you will conclude that mastery of a discipline, or technical ability, was *not* the decisive factor. Rather, the qualities that most frequently differentiate the top performers from others are the intangibles of creativity, persistence, follow-through, attention to detail, empathy, and so on.

Reliable and steady organizational activity depends on the merging of diverse talents and ideas. Diversity allows organizations to avoid mindless collective action and the harmful convergence of opinion. In the hive, a subset of bees—not all or none—will act as conditions dictate in order to create a proper balance (e.g., of temperature). Variability among individual bees is precisely what keeps the colony from doing too little or too much.

LESSON 14

DISCOVER AND USE THE SPECIALIZED
TALENTS OF YOUR EMPLOYEES

D iversity is indispensable to organizations in ways
other than the promotion of stability. For instance,
individual differences in sensitivity to environmental
cues, such as the sweetness of nectar, lead bees to specialize
in different tasks. The same principle operates in our household. My mother-in-law lives with us and she always cleans
the kitchen; we might say that is one of her specialties. Why
does she do it and we—the other members of our family—
don't? The truth of the matter is that she can't stand having
dirty dishes lying about, while the rest of us are perfectly
content to watch the stacks grow before we're forced to
intervene. One or two members of our family unit would, in
fact, never clean the kitchen if not politely asked. But it's
these differential thresholds to various aspects of our environment that make the household work: the dogs get walked,
the weeds get pulled, dinners get made, clothes get washed,

the bills get paid, and so on because we have enough people around who are willing and able to do different things. We have a colony of specialists, and operations in the home wouldn't be as effective if we were all the same.

Efficiency requires that the work of the group has been subdivided into meaningful parts or activities, that time and effort have been allocated to activities appropriately, and that those who are responsible for fulfilling such activities are the ones best suited for each job. It wouldn't be constructive for all of the worker bees to morph into a single type of bee that could perform only one job. Fortunately, this will never occur, thanks to the workers' dissimilar sensory abilities that make them more or less apt to assume certain jobs. For example, bees differ in their threshold for detecting sucrose, their favorite type of sugar in nectar. Scientists have demonstrated that some bees will react to very low levels of sucrose as evidenced when the bees stick out their slender, hairy, strawlike tongues when the taste hairs on their antennae are stimulated. Other bees will respond only to very sweet solutions. These differences in sensitivity to tastes—as well as to odors and light—make certain bees more fit to do certain jobs. Bees who are the least receptive to external stimuli (e.g., taste), for example, become nectar foragers. Given that nectar has a naturally sugary taste, finely tuned senses are not required to detect it. The greatest sensitivity is required for substances without much allure such as water and, consequently, the most discerning bees become water foragers. Honeybees with intermediate sensitivities become pollen foragers. Therefore, workers forage according to their unique sensory abilities that make each one best at a particular search and collection task.

Sensory differences appear at an early age among workers, but thresholds can be modified by environmental conditions such as humidity, season, and the nutritional status within the hive. This plasticity enables the honeybee to make behavioral corrections depending on the circumstances, versus committing to a fixed number of water, pollen, and nectar foragers. A flexible division of labor allows them to appropriately react to changes in conditions. Similarly, if my mother-in-law was out of town and our family ran out of clean plates, we all might become more willing to pitch in and wash a dish or two, thereby demonstrating our adaptive competence and eminence in the animal kingdom.

Self-discovery about work preferences, and selecting and matching people to jobs, is really about understanding and acknowledging that individuals have different thresholds for particular tasks. These thresholds may reflect differences in preferences, capabilities, or both. People will accomplish more and better work if a set of activities are aligned well with individuals' strengths and weaknesses, preferences and tolerances. Ideally, a company will structure jobs so that each position has a relatively homogeneous set of elements attached to it, as opposed to far-fetched sets of tasks. A bad job design is one that includes dissimilar tasks that one person couldn't humanly perform or would have no conceivable interest in performing. Nevertheless, given that even the best jobs contain aspects that incumbents may find poor matches to their skills or interests, it might be beneficial to shuffle some activities around within a team. For example, some tasks can be separated into pieces so that the mismatched elements could be performed by those for whom the match is better. People who hate details, for example, can surround themselves with those who are better suited to organization.

In our preoccupation with A-players, we sometimes discount contributions that may appear to have little direct impact on the total company, failing to see that all sorts of performances interact to make organizations better. An excellent employee with relatively low rank can make a star's light shine brighter. When hiring, then, it is important to know not only the skills and competencies of the new recruit but the abilities of other individuals in the current workforce in order to decide if and how a new employee will fit into the mix. This avoids unnecessary redundancies and facilitates meaningful interactions among organizational members. Think of yourself as building a Fellowship of the Ring, that unlikely band that saves Middle Earth in J.R.R. Tolkien's fantasy trilogy, *The Lord of the Rings*. The fellowship is made up of members of multiple races (e.g., hobbits, elves, humans). Each member can do what the others cannot. Elves, for example, counter spells and hobbits trick monsters. It is their special blend of differences that makes them successful. The fitness of the hive depends upon diversity. Colonies that are more diverse are better at rearing the young, comb building, and collecting and storing food. And because a diverse colony has wide reactions to environmental cues, the colony can take advantage of a broader range of food sources. The distribution of information about the whereabouts of food is wider and more complete, making the hive as a whole more effective. Conversely, a more homogeneous colony may forage within a certain geographic range of the hive and only from flowers with very high nectar levels—thereby reducing their chances for success.

More Pollen

The colony's ability to allocate labor in a way that is consistent with the hive's needs is one of the colony's most distinctive qualities. Honeybees have a knack for deploying themselves in the right numbers and right ways to produce their yields. They can do this well because they have a diverse workforce that at any given time contains bees at different levels of maturity who are able to fulfill different functions under varied conditions. In essence, it's a matter of making the proper placements of a highly specialized group. The situational fit of talent is critical to performance.

It is a wonderful feeling when a team "clicks." Every manager knows the satisfaction of having the right people with the right complement of skills and temperaments that contribute to the team's success. In contrast, when teams do not fulfill their potential, often it is because the mix of talents and assignments is not quite right. Rather than falsely conclude, then, that low performance must be due to lack of ability or effort, it is worth exploring the possibility that an employee has been poorly cast. As in a jazz band, we should question whether a person is occupying the right role within the group and whether others are helping that person play his or her best before we assume the worst. The most pragmatic advice I can offer is to take the time to get to know what your people are capable of doing, which skill gaps exist across people, and who in the immediate organization may be instrumental to others' development.

LESSON 15

DEVELOP YOUR TEAM

Bees are a disciplined lot. Each bee goes through an orderly developmental progression that is linked to both individual ability and hive needs. Bees move through a series of age-related jobs that can be modified by social context and colony requirements. Practically speaking, bees' development can be accelerated, slowed, or even reversed based on the external conditions and needs of the colony.

Honeybee development follows the adage "When children are young, give them roots; when they grow, give them wings." Their work life begins with the safest, easiest jobs within the hive and advances to the most difficult, hazardous jobs outside the hive. The first jobs of workers are in the deepest recesses of the nest, cleaning cells and capping brood (baby bees). They quickly graduate to "nurse" bees, which are responsible for feeding the larvae and caring for the queen. As they reach middle age, they move closer to the periphery of the hive and are engaged in comb building, cleaning out debris, and receiving nectar. Bees also have a dual career path that becomes available at about this time. Honeybees can become either guards or undertakers. The latter, as the title suggests, remove corpses from the hive and the former stand near the hive entrance, vigilantly protecting the hive from intruders.

Actually, the guards will survey the area around the hive and harass poachers that get too close. Unfortunately, I learned this fact through firsthand experience. As I gathered honey one day, I soon discovered that my old borrowed head veil had a small hole. I can tell you that having "a bee in your bonnet" is not a good thing, particularly because there is never just one bee. The first bee to sting summons others by emitting a pheromone that smells a bit like bananas, and thrashing about doesn't frighten them away. This particular outing to the hive resulted in multiple stings to my head before I could extricate myself from the situation. (Not wishing to have a similar experience in the future, I called my inventive brother-in-law Bill, who promptly sent me one of his UltraBreeze Bee Suits made of an airy mesh that bees cannot penetrate.)

After about three weeks, many workers are ready to leave home and take flight as foragers that specialize in collecting different materials needed by the colony. Some bees gather pollen as the sole protein source, some gather nectar as the raw material for honey, some gather water to dilute the honey and cool the hive, and others gather a resinous material from trees (propolis) to seal cracks in the hive.

The life trajectories of the hive's members are affected by

circumstance. For example, if there is a shortage of nurse bees, the job progression is delayed so that more nurse bees are available to care for the young. If the shortage is extreme, foragers may even pitch in as "reverted nurses." On the other hand, if foragers are desperately needed, then the pace of development quickens to the point where bees as young as five to seven days old are prepared to venture out from the hive.

What does the developmental progression of bees tell us about how employees might be trained and given opportunities through corporate career programs? What works? I have been in hundreds of companies and, unfortunately, the majority of career development programs receive little funding or institutional attention. The result is programs that function in name only. The success of honeybees, however, suggests elements of a career development program that is truly worthy of the name. Taking the lead from bees, stellar development programs have the following components:

Connect to staffing plans

- While career development affects individuals, successful programs are embedded in a company-wide system that is attuned to the company's goals and resources. In the hive, bees' developmental progressions and movements are stimulated by colony need. What occurs in an individual case is partly the result of context. Similarly, career and human-resource professionals should have information at their disposal about how many people are needed, when they are needed, where they are needed, and how vacancies or developmental holes are to be filled.

Set behavioral criteria for advancement/job performance

• No bee is born a forager. Its physiology and sensory capabilities aren't equipped for the task. Sending the bee out into the world before it is ready would result in certain death. Older bees keep younger bees from venturing forth too soon by emitting a chemical that prevents these teen equivalents from busting loose. In a similar manner, to assure that employees will succeed at progressively difficult jobs, it is essential to define the competencies required to perform the job well at each step in a career ladder. Employees, then, understand what they need to master in order to advance, and those entrusted with employees' development know which training exercises and opportunities are needed to foster growth. The entire process is transparent, predictable, and motivational.

Allow for multiple pathways

• Good career progressions have branches that allow employees to follow different paths according to their inclinations and talents. Not everyone will excel at what the company initially anticipated. Good career programs give people options so that both employees and companies can explore the kinds of positions that best suit employees' capabilities.

Actively promote growth experiences

• In a good development program, employees are assisted by growth-related initiatives sponsored by the company, including formal and informal training. In the hive, bees are trained for certain difficult chores such as foraging and improve as a result. Novice foragers are more likely to follow veteran foragers into the field, whereas experienced foragers tend to follow others only when they have been unsuccessful. Through observation and practice, bees increase their nectar loads. They learn to improve their navigation, become more discriminating about flowers, and manipulate flowers more effectively to extract nectar. As with bees, people are not born accomplished. The best companies will devote resources to quickening the rate at which employees become proficient on the job so that workers have longer periods of productivity.

Provide broad exposure to varied tasks

• Bees have a varied career. Their short histories include exposure to different functional tasks, opportunities to be lead bees on important hive missions, and substantial job variability, as when foragers occupy themselves with other colony tasks when not needed in the field. We would describe a person who has followed a similar developmental route as well informed, well rounded, and fortunate. The complex corporate program that would enable this sort of movement would be highly organized, attentive, and forward thinking.

More Pollen

One of the most important things you can do to enhance organizational performance is to implement intelligent career development programs. Following the multifaceted system exhibited by bees, sound employee development occurs along three axes. One is an *upward* developmental trajectory with progressively more challenging jobs and increasing responsibilities. This refers to traditional career programs in which managers base advancement decisions on the maturing abilities and experiences of employees, and demonstrated excellence on successively higher-order tasks. Two, development can be *inward*, where growth is promoted in the job through increased proficiency. In this instance, managers, in tandem with the employee, identify in-role opportunities to sharpen the employee's particular abilities or deepen his or her knowledge base. This is achieved through on-the-job training, seminars, and other educational methods designed to improve one or more dimensions of current performance. Third, development can be *outward* through exposure to lateral jobs that allow employees to acquire different skill sets. A manager, for example, can assign an employee to a project team in which the employee will be exposed to new methods or technologies or formally move her to a new functional area where she will acquire new but related skills. An effective, comprehensive career system is one that increases employees' breadth and depth of knowledge.

CORKSCREW LEARNING

Clearly, animals have to learn in order to adapt. Some of this learning can't await instruction from others or accommodate a lengthy period of knowledge acquisition. The learning must be done on the spot and at the learner's own initiative. This is not a small matter since a little bit of initiative and active engagement with one's surroundings can go a very long way.

Honeybees, as it happens, are active learners. They practice what might be called turn-back-and-look learning (TBL Learning). When honeybees turn back and look, they are attending to features in their environment that will enable them to return to a site without getting lost. We do the same when visiting unfamiliar places. In order to find our way back home, we look for clues such as a roadway fruit stand, a car sitting on blocks in a driveway, or a crossroad.

The stimulus for active learning in honeybees is novelty and change, such as a new forage site or a sudden alteration in conditions that predict the quality of a nectar source. In situations such as these, the bees want to be sure they will be able to retrace their path and, therefore, they perform learning flights to acquaint themselves with the terrain below them. These learning flights follow a corkscrew pattern that spirals upward, expanding in radius as the bees' elevations increase.

The effectiveness of active learning is apparent in honeybees. Consider one experiment by Wei and Dyer in which bees, enclosed in a flight cage, were presented with an octagonal table containing artificial flowers. One flower on the table contained sucrose syrup and the remaining flowers were decoys. The diagram shows the basic setup. It is a simple matter for bees to locate the food source, but, as they feed, the table is rotated 180 degrees so that the place of departure is opposite their place of arrival.

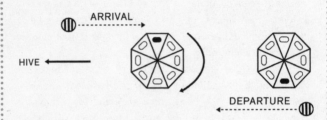

Diagram 3 Turn-back-and-look Active Learning

ADAPTED FROM WEI, C. A., AND DYER, F. C. (2009). "INVESTING IN LEARNING: WHY DO HONEYBEES, *APIS MELLIFERA*, VARY THE DURATIONS OF LEARNING FLIGHTS?" *ANIMAL BEHAVIOUR* 77, 1165–1177. REPRINTED BY PERMISSION OF ELSEVIER.

When bees return to the table for more sucrose, they won't want to go to where the sucrose was found, but to where it was last seen—their place of departure. Given that the sucrose-filled flower had been spatially reoriented, the bees' search will be error-plagued if they don't examine the departure site with a new intensity through learning flights. In fact, the researchers found that the length of the learning flights was related to accuracy in landing at the departure flower on the subsequent trip.

A little self-study saves time and increases performance. It is nice to have well-designed instructional programs in companies but they can't totally replace all forms of learning, especially the will to learn and grow on one's own. If something seems odd or out of place or puzzling, an employee who is curious enough to explore what might be amiss on his or her own is worth gold. On the other hand, organizations where the employees wait to be told will have a hard time surviving.

LESSON 16

OUTCOMPETE BY OUTFINESSING RIVALS

From its humble beginnings in Africa and Eurasia, the honeybee now has a worldwide presence. In fact, the honeybee's presence has spread to such an extent that some naturalists have characterized it as "invasive." When the honeybee enters the local flower market, it usually takes over.

Honeybees are the Wal-Mart of the insect kingdom: nifty, ever-present competitors. They are generalist invaders, feeding on more than one hundred species of plants in a given geographic area, laying claim to the vast riches of their territory. Although they are not particularly hostile insects, they will push around smaller insects that get in their way and intimidate smaller birds, such as humming-birds. Honeybees, in fact, can sting other insects without killing themselves in the process. However, stinging mam-mals, including us, is another story. The harpoon-shaped barb at the end of the stinger catches under our tough skins and the bee yanks its insides out as it tries to remove the stinger (and venom sac). A common misconception is that bees die immediately after stinging us, but they can continue to badger any intruders for up to two additional days before succumbing to their injuries. I suspect that this little problem with the honeybee's stinger will find an evolutionary remedy in due time as humans become increasingly "invasive."

Honeybees consistently outperform one of the chief rivals, the bumblebee, through greater agility in the collection of nectar. Think of the logistical abilities of a company like the Spanish retailer Zara. Consider the way Zara defeats competitors by putting new designs into showrooms within two weeks of concept creation—versus the industry average of nine months—and you will get an intuitive feel for the honeybees' approach.

Honeybees and bumblebees have overlapping market interests of 50 percent or more, and honeybees are able to push bumblebees to the territorial fringes by systematically co-opting supply. Although scientists debate the specific effects of honeybees on bumblebee populations, they agree that honeybees are formidable competitors. Even if they do not outright squash the competition, honeybees gradually reduce the bumblebees' fitness by forcing their rival to alter its foraging behaviors, including sending smaller, less effective bumblebees into the field. Forcing change in competitors' behavior is a highly prized form of competitive advantage. In essence, the competition is submitting to a rival's strategies, and often in ways that are detrimental to the competitors' own success. For example, bumblebees may be compelled to reduce their harvesting range or extend their harvesting hours. As a result, they may not find the variety of flowers they need or may encounter new predators and competitors for which they are poorly equipped to cope.

The remarkable success of the honeybee is attributable to several factors discussed in the prior lessons. Over the years I have spent learning about the social life of bees, I have tested and confirmed the applicability of my insights to business with countless professionals and leaders in companies of various sizes and industries. A few of the more important lessons for competitive advantage to bear in mind are these:

Set clear goals and direction

- What needs to be done, and by what time, is clear in the hive. The brood needs so much pollen intake daily, and the honey stores need to be built up to certain levels before the temperature turns cold.

Define assignments and accountability

- Honeybees have mastered division of labor and each bee has a specific task it is responsible for carrying out. Actually, accountabilities are even more precise than I have described elsewhere, since some foragers may temporarily specialize in certain types of flowers.

Practice active discovery

- Although honeybees concentrate their resources at the most productive sites, the inquisitive bee continues to scout out new bounty through exploratory flights. As a result, they are continuously on the lookout for new profitable patches to harvest.

Encourage learning

- Honeybees' proficiency at being in the right place at the right time is partly due to their ability to associate the types and locations of flowers with the times of day in which the flowers offer their greatest yields. The hive contains a reservoir of information about its external environment, permitting the colony to begin each day with awareness of the days that came before. Their ability to learn keeps honeybees current and attentive to what matters most within their field of activity.

Build effective teamwork

- Notably selfless at the colony level, honeybees also spontaneously form teams that assemble and dissolve like those that occur in consultancies. For example, when a profitable flower patch is discovered, many of the same recruits will harvest it together—forming a dedicated group that already knows how to efficiently get to and from the patch and is familiar with the flowers within it.

Leave some room for enterprise

- Honeybees use several pathways to exchange information in order to monitor hive status and external conditions. Importantly, the best communications are not always the most exact. The information about the location of flowers provided by scout bees is often approximate—it gets recruits close but recruits have to sniff their way around from there. The scout is like a good manager who refrains from telling an employee in excruciating detail precisely how to do a task. In the end, the result may be something much better than originally imagined.

Empower others

- Opportunities are fleeting in the wild, and the winners get to nature's goods first. For all of the honeybees' wonderful abilities, they would not succeed if they failed to have the right proportion of workers deployed in the right jobs or if they failed to mobilize them quickly. The bees' highly decentralized form of government allows the workers who are closest to the information to act upon it immediately and make the most informed decisions.

The honeybees' success really is quite amazing when you stop to think about it. Thousands of nest mates perform a portfolio of jobs and coordinate their actions in a highly cohesive way. Now, why can't we do that more routinely? If we were to ascribe a cultural identity to bees that gives them an edge in the wild, three qualities would stand out. Bees exhibit a worldview that we correspondingly would describe as fair, open-minded, and objective.

BE FAIR.

First, the hive treats every foraging bee as equally important. It does not matter which bee finds the nectar. Others will look to the discoverer for guidance and many will choose to follow. Although some honeybees may be predisposed to become scouts (a debatable contention within the research community), honeybees display a cool indifference to which of the many bees contribute the most at any given time. There is no wrestling for credit, no backstabbing, undermining, or usurping—just a celebratory sipping of honey in the winter when they all have enough to drink.

BE OPEN-MINDED.

Second, honeybees do not prematurely close off discourse when presented with facts contrary to their recent experiences. For example, after the bees have fully exploited the nectar of a flower patch, they abandon the patch but periodically check back for a few hours just to make sure that circumstances have not changed. Later, however, they may observe a scout bee that is directing them back to the very place that they previously abandoned. They do not gaze skeptically at the scout as if to suggest, "We've been to that spot, and there is nothing there," a.k.a., "We've done that before and it doesn't work." They visit the site to see for themselves, knowing that their prior assessment may no longer apply. They don't immediately commit to the redis-covered patch, but they will investigate. We could say that honeybees remain open to possibilities even if on the surface the options presented seem implausible. In the hive, there is no reason to distrust what others are saying.

BE OBJECTIVE AND DATA-DRIVEN.

Third, the decisions bees ultimately make are evidence-based. There is no cult of personality in the hive such that Hector-the-Nectar-Collector is always right and must be obeyed. The real guide for colonies is data, supported by an uncanny attention to detail. They would get lost in a confusing, colorful sea of flora otherwise. As honeybees leave the hive each morning, they must find the most productive flower patches at the lowest transactional costs including travel and handling times (the time it takes to extract nectar). Innate preferences and experience combine to inform foragers' decisions, reducing the problem space with which they must deal. Consequently, honeybees attend to the relevant physical attributes of flowers that correlate with nectar quantities. They favor flowers that are larger, of particular colors, unblemished (and therefore never robbed), and symmetrical in shape. In this way, they are able to attend to clusters of flowers that are most likely to be profitable. Similarly, they are able to avoid those that are of lower value, assisted by a pruning strategy by which honeybees mark flowers they have tapped in order to eliminate visits by others to depleted sources (bees leave trace hydrocarbons on flowers that can be sensed by other bees). Honeybees also tend to stick with the same or similar flowers as they harvest. This provides bees with the dual advantage of harvesting from a source that is known to have high yields while minimizing the flight distances between plants, since the same plants tend to be found in clusters.

Overall, the abilities of honeybees are highly refined. For example, they will feed on three-day-old capitula in the early morning and two-day-old capitula later in the day. Their scavenging is not perfect, but for those unfortunate insects that wish to share the honeybees' domain, it is extremely efficient. In many respects, the honeybees' formula for success should be no surprise to businesspeople. Clear goals and accountabilities, for example, are staples of enterprise. What distinguishes honeybees is that they actually do the very things we know we should.

More Pollen

Have you ever noticed that at first there is one bee drinking from your open can of orange soda, then soon there are two, three, four. . . . The collective speed and effectiveness of honeybees depends on their constant intake and use of information. They are fast, very fast, and that makes them able competitors.

Since I already have expounded in this chapter on what you should do to be a quick, responsive competitor, I will concentrate here on what you should not do. Successful adaptation not only requires taking effective actions, but modifying or eliminating ineffective ones.

Elting Morison (historian and founder of MIT's Program in Science, Technology, and Society) recounts one of my favorite stories in his book *Men, Machines, and Modern Times*. A time and motion expert once filmed a British artillery crew of five during the Second World War and noticed that two members of the crew inexplicably ceased activity and came to attention for a period lasting the duration of the discharge of the field cannon. As it happens, their posture was the one taken during the First World War by two members of an artillery crew who held their tethered horses in place. During the Second World War, the horses were long gone but the old processes remained.

Honeybees' constant intake and use of information make them fast and formidable competitors. They use data quickly and effectively in order to react to opportunities and shed themselves of wasted motions and obsolete functions. If a company wishes to be equally responsive and nimble—and which company wouldn't—then they must self-consciously take in new information and put it to good use. But it takes effort to stop what you're doing, and that is why I find the simple prescription of Joshua Ehrlich, an experienced executive coach, to be refreshing. In order to lift oneself out of a rut (that becomes a grave as it grows deeper and wider), he recommends taking the following three steps: stop, reflect, focus. The basic idea is that reflection, the ability to examine ourselves and deliberate on our actions, is an intentional act that involves a willingness to disengage from the habitual and to reassess our direction in the context of core purposes and values.

IT LOOKS A LOT LIKE TRUST

Over the years, researchers have conducted what have been referred to as "lake experiments." The question addressed is whether forager bees will follow dancers to an implausible location in the middle of a lake. That is, will bees reject the dances of nest mates that signal places that are unlikely to yield food?

In one experiment, Wray and her colleagues trained bees to locate feeders equidistant from a test hive. One set of bees was trained to find a feeder on land and another set was trained to find a feeder on an anchored boat on a lake 260 meters from shore. The diagram shows the basic design.

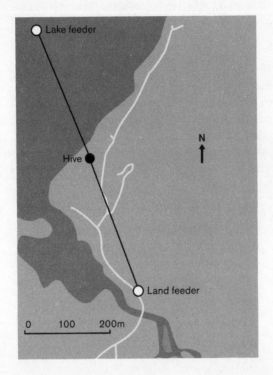

Diagram 4 Trust Me: Land or Water

ADAPTED FROM WRAY, M. K., KLEIN, B. A., MATTILA, H. R., AND SEELEY, T. D. (2008). "HONEYBEES DO NOT REJECT DANCES FOR 'IMPLAUSIBLE' LOCATIONS: RECONSIDERING THE EVIDENCE FOR COGNITIVE MAPS IN INSECTS." *ANIMAL BEHAVIOUR* 76, 261–269. REPRINTED BY PERMISSION OF ELSEVIER.

As it happens, the bees' dance was the same whether advertising for food on land or water, and followers were as likely to leave the hive in search of the food regardless of the feeder's location. Furthermore, followers were as likely to appear at the feeder on the lake as they were at the feeder on land.

One explanation for these results is that bees lack a type of intelligence: they are unable to form mental representations or maps of their surrounds and, therefore, do not recognize dances that are leading in an implausible direction. Actually, none of the lake experiments to date has been able to make this conclusion. It is just as likely that bees have a clear sensory image of where they are heading but have no reason to suspect their sisters of lying. Given that all members of the hive want the same things, when a bee is advocating for something that potentially will help the colony, why not listen? In organizations, we would call honest communications sincerely spoken and faithfully received and acted upon as trust.

LESSON 17

PREPARE FOR LEADERSHIP CHANGES

Bank of America illustrates how quickly corporate fortunes can change. It also illustrates the importance of succession planning. When CEO Kenneth Lewis suddenly announced his retirement on September 30, 2009 (with a retirement date set for December 31, 2009), the board had no ready replacement. Consequently, newspaper accounts have described the transition as "tense" and as a poor time (in the midst of a recession) to be between leaders and adrift.

Queens are replaced in one of two ways—naturally from the inside through a process called "supercedure" or artificially from the outside. When it occurs from the outside, the beekeeper introduces a new queen in a process known as "re-queening." Therefore, either an insider or an outsider can fill the most important position in the hive.

A colony headed by a high-quality queen has a more robust worker population and greater honey yield. It matters a great deal who is at the top. Consequently, it is not surprising that the workers in the hive pay close attention to the queen's ability to propagate and are sensitive to declines in her performance. The queen's ability to lead is determined ultimately by the minions, a truth unfortunately lost in many organizations. Leadership depends on the consent of the people to follow. In the instance of bees, the voice of workers is loud and clear.

When the workers detect a drop-off in the queen's productivity, they quickly begin to plan for a successor. The planning begins even while the queen is still performing adequately, not when she can no longer lay eggs. The bees realize that the end of her most productive phase is approaching and that they need to begin preparations for a replacement. In contrast to honeybees' conscientiousness, more than 40 percent of companies have no succession plan in place for their executives, according to an estimate from the National Association of Corporate Directors.

Honeybees have a deep, innate concern for succession since the colony will not survive without a queen. Even a significant decline in the queen's egg-laying capacity would threaten the hive. As a result, the colony must take steps to develop a replacement while the hive is still in good health. The fact is, grooming a successor takes a long time. It takes sixteen days to develop a queen, an additional six days for her to reach sexual maturity, and another week before she begins to lay well. So, if a colony has to start from scratch in replacing a queen (emergency queen rearing), the colony will have experienced the better part of a month when no eggs will have been laid and no young workers produced. This would be a huge setback for a colony, especially in spring.

For a business example, consider the anxieties within Apple and the investment community when Steve Jobs stepped away from the company for health-related reasons. The loss of any CEO can be traumatic when there is no suitable Plan B in place, but it can be especially so when a person and company are synonymous, as Jobs and Apple are. In fact, Apple's share prices have moved in direct relation to Jobs's comings and goings, rising when he shows up and falling when he has temporarily withdrawn.

Fate can abruptly strike companies from many different directions and leave them leaderless. Alfred Herrhausen, the CEO of Deutsche Bank, was assassinated by a bomb in 1989. Jim Cantalupo of McDonald's died of a heart attack and his replacement died of cancer soon afterward. Siemens suddenly lost its CEO, Klaus Kleinfeld, during a period when the company was enmeshed in a bribery scandal. Unless a company has a planned successor to bring forward in an emergency, the company must endure a period of great uncertainty and the embarrassment of being unprepared for a business contingency it could have anticipated—not the sort of thing that comforts employees and shareholders. Particularly inexcusable is when an executive has advised the company of his or her impending retirement and yet nothing is done. Although former CEO Douglas Daft of Coca-Cola notified the board five years in advance of his retirement, the company seemed to be caught unaware, resulting in a high-profile botch job that left Coca-Cola rudderless and the press plenty to write about.

All of the females of the hive begin life as equals—as eggs fertilized by the queen. The queen lays approximately one to two dozen eggs in roomier cells reserved for the larger queens. Then, as in Huxley's *Brave New World*, the workers apply special compounds to the growing cells at select times to promote the differentiation of the cells into a queen. She is born with possibility, but relies on the dedicated nurturing of workers to fully mature into a sovereign. In particular, workers (nurse bees) raise queens on a special, quality diet of what is known as royal jelly, consisting of higher concentrations of glucose and fructose (among other things) than the brood food fed to future workers. Even in the hive, no one who achieves greatness ascends without the selfless assistance of others.

When a hive needs only one queen to replace the reigning queen, the new queen will be the one who has advanced the furthest the fastest. The most mature, prepared queen gets the job. Queens develop in phases that every grade-schooler learns: egg, five larval stages, pupa, and adult. In the final larval stage, the bee spins itself a cocoon and the worker bees cap the cell with a porous wax lid. The first queen to emerge from a cell has almost a two-to-one chance of becoming the next queen. This nascent queen dispatches her rivals who have not yet emerged by stinging them through the walls of their queen cells, achieving supremacy over her helpless sisters and half sisters in less than two days. There is only one leader in the hive and this bit of business assures that it stays that way with minimal expenditure of time and conflict. These are quick, ritualistic assassinations and by no means "fights." The workers pretty much stay out of the way and allow these events to unfold as they likely have for millions of years.

Since the new queen will be vulnerable to dangers as she begins her mating flights, the colony keeps the old queen on until the new queen has mated and successfully returned to the hive to begin her work. Thus, after a successor emerges, the incumbent stays on during a brief transition period before completely ceding power. A comparable general strategy in corporations entails progressively giving a successor more space, with the incumbent CEO remaining available as needed but continuously stepping back until she is completely out of the way. For example, a former CEO may temporarily stay on as chairman as Michael Critelli did at Pitney Bowes and Charles Holliday has done at DuPont while ceding executive powers to Murray Martin and Ellen Kullman, respectively. Leadership transitions have similarly proceeded smoothly at other institutions, including PepsiCo (Reinemund to Nooyi) and Wal-Mart (Scott to Duke). Warning: Boards of directors sometimes have difficulty with an arrangement in which a former CEO spends too much time as chairperson, fearing that the predecessor CEO is too close for comfort and may stifle free discussion.

If the old queen has sense, she will retreat to some corner of the hive and live out her years in peace—with emeritus status. Lacking good sense, she is eliminated. Scientists do not really know how long past and future queens coexist, nor are they certain who eliminates the mother queen following succession. However, when the transition is complete, one leader remains.

There have been corporate instances of successful twin leaders in organizations—Aéropostale, RIM, and J.M. Smucker, to name a few—but these arrangements are short-lived and tend to work as long as responsibilities and resources are neatly segregated (for example, one person handles merchandising, the other handles operations) and the temperaments of the incumbents permit power sharing. These are big ifs and they seldom materialize in the workplace. Reality often undoes these utopian ideals. Coleaders frequently are individuals who started companies together and are accustomed to working with one another. More often, organizations with dual leaders produce mixed messages, divided loyalties, and interpersonal conflicts. Dual leadership is not impossible, but the myriad conditions for peaceful coexistence make it implausible. Take it from the hive—one leader is more than enough.

The highly visible, tempestuous relationship between Sandy Weill and John Reed at Citigroup in the late nineties, which eventually led to Reed's ouster, is much more representative of the two-headed monsters I have seen in organizations. The unfortunate situation of having coleaders of departments and business units usually has a common cause: a higher authority failed to choose between two candidates for the wrong reasons of appeasement and cowardice. If you ever find yourself needing to choose between candidates, please do yourself and everyone else a favor and make a decision.

As it happens, there are occasions when more than one job opens up for a queen. Sometimes after a colony swarms, there are secondary swarms, or "afterswarms." In addition to needing a new queen for the hive (the original queen leaves with the main swarm), the afterswarm needs a new queen. In this case, the workers cannot stand by and watch the first queen emerge to immediately kill all her rivals, since at least two survivors will be required. The workers, therefore, avoid this by grabbing, clamping, and chasing the queens, prohibiting rivals from immediately killing one another off. As a result, several potential successors are able to emerge from their cells. One queen will accompany the afterswarm. Another surviving queen will stay in the home nest and inherit the rich resources of the hive.

Two observations stand out from these queen duels. First, workers care who wins the duel and it is clear that they influence the results. The outcomes of these fights are not chance events. It is not yet clear why workers favor one queen over another, but, aside from this mystery, the behavior of workers illustrates that it is helpful to have a few well-placed friends who can bias the proceedings. It is an obvious point but a useful reminder for all aspiring corporate climbers that it is far better to make friends on the way up than enemies. It is noteworthy, however, that the bees never appear to support a queen who is not fit for office.

Second, since the fisticuffs occur between females, a question that may arise is, "Isn't it just like women to kill each other off?" It's a disturbing question, I know, and one I reluctantly raise as the pink elephant in the room. The stinging abuse sometimes inflicted by women on women has been colorfully portrayed in the novel (and movie) *The Devil Wears Prada*, and cataloged by author Susan Shapiro Barash in *Tripping the Prom Queen*—a work based on interviews with five hundred women. Many female managers have told me about the rivalry among their "sisters" over the years. Expecting encouragement and support from one another, they feel bitten instead. Indeed, there is some survey evidence that suggests that male, bully managers tend to be equal-opportunity brutes but women tend to pick on their own. If this is true (and I don't know if it is), I can wager a guess that it is for the same reason infighting occurs among bees—there is a quota system in place. Many are called but few are chosen, and the options faced by bees are not particularly attractive. If they surrender, they die. If they leave in an afterswarm, there is an 80 percent chance of expiring by the end of their first winter (parental colonies have an 80 percent chance of surviving winters). The most appealing position is as surviving queen in the home colony.

When a company "reserves" a certain number of important positions for women, the company is expressly creating a condition of scarcity and fostering a tournament mentality of winners and losers. Anytime an organization suggests, "We need two women on the board" or "We need two female officers in the company," an implicit quota system is established. The company is proposing a target that is greater in number than the company might otherwise have had, but also less than they might otherwise have if they truly considered merit. This is a plausible thesis given the underrepresentation of women on boards of directors and officer-level positions within Fortune 500 companies. About 15 percent of women are members of boards and are officers in large public companies (the percentages are lower within the top hundred companies on the London Exchange). Yet women make up around 50 percent of the managerial and professional workforce. The problem of disproportion is complex, but at least part of the solution is simple. Attend to the developmental interests of all parties and promote the best people irrespective of their outward characteristics.

Some people may hold themselves back from advancement because something akin to a queen duel is anathema to their self-image and value system that prizes humility over ambition. I tell talented people who shun ambition because of its negative implications that there is nothing wrong with being ambitious and working hard for what they want for themselves. As long as they, men and women alike, respect the collective goals of the organization, they need not fret over those who are envious of their achievements and make disparaging remarks. No apologies are required for performing well and being successful.

More Pollen

If the honeybee teaches us anything, it is that organizations cannot survive without a leader and, therefore, the colony prevents costly voids in leadership by planning for successors in advance of the obvious need. Colonies die without their top bee; organizations become pathological sans leadership.

Although honeybees essentially nominate the first in line for high office, bear in mind what they are trying to do: find a productive replacement queen with as little contention and internal disruption as possible. This works well in the hive since the first bee out of its cell usually is fit to be queen. This is not necessarily true in companies. The person who has been around the longest may not be the best performer currently or the best equipped to meet future circumstances and institutional needs.

Despite the operation of the powerful norm of first in, first up, do not count on its use to quell dissent since it is not a neutral promotional criterion. It favors time over performance and can saddle organizations with certain kinds of people depending on who tends to stay. The company that assures that the best will prevail is the one that will attract and retain a more diverse, competent population.

Although this lesson may appear to pertain to the executive ranks, the replacement of managers and key employees is an issue throughout organizations. If you lose a manager who is integral to operations, the organization will feel the effects if the position remains vacant. Filling highly skilled jobs requires as much thought and preparation as replenishing executive openings. To ensure that a replacement is ready, managers should increasingly expose internal candidates to the core duties of their jobs so possible successors are somewhat practiced should they be called upon. Planning for one's own succession is not an easy thing to do. In fact, many managers resist giving direct reports too much entrée to their work, fearing that the access will lead to the manager's demise. This, however, dampens the overall level of expertise within the organization. A confident leader who progressively develops those beneath her will ensure her team's continued success and her own advancement.

LESSON 18

BRING IN NEW BLOOD FOR NEW LIFE

Given the great demands placed upon the queen, her life is never easy or safe, but it is particularly difficult and dangerous for an externally imposed queen. In fact, rejection rates of new queens are estimated to be as high as 50 percent. Newly hired outside executives have similarly high failure rates. As we will see, introducing new leadership requires great care in order to improve the chance of success.

The beekeeper introduces a new queen when it becomes clear that something about the current colony lineage is putting the colony at risk. Most often, the problem is susceptibility to disease, but the colony also may have developed strong, unfavorable traits such as aggressiveness, uncleanliness, and infirmity. The hive is in trouble and the colony needs new leadership to introduce a new strain and culture.

When organizations choose to go outside the institution for replacements, they send the message to markets and employees that they lack suitable internal candidates who can adequately perform the necessary duties. Change is needed and the new leader has the unenviable disadvantage of being the one who is asked to do what the organization (or business unit, division, or department) could not do for itself.

The decision to replace a key position with an external hire requires a certain degree of nonpartisanship and objectivity that can be difficult for people within a troubled system to achieve. In fact, colonies that are passing on negative traits don't liberate themselves: the beekeeper does. Similarly, companies rely on the independence of boards of directors to assess whether or not the requisite executive talent exists within the company. The same heavy responsibility rests with managers throughout the organization who must make the decisions to promote from within or go outside.

Going outside the hive or tribe upsets the natural order of social systems that seek to confer benefits within the "family" or society. This heightens fear among employees that the outsider will pose a threat to the organization because he or she does not understand how it has operated in the past and will implement unwanted changes to the existing order. Perhaps for this reason, companies with tightly knit and friendly boards and senior management teams prefer to play it safe by sticking with known entities, as General Motors initially did in making Fritz Henderson the successor CEO to Rick Wagoner. The danger, of course, is that an insider may not be able to recast an ossified culture and effectively correct course. Think how Peter Löscher must have felt when he took the reins of Siemens as the first outsider CEO in the company's 162-year history in the wake of a paralyzing scandal. My palms sweat just thinking about it.

The welcoming committee for outsiders can be quite hostile, as it certainly is within the hive. Introducing a young bee as queen of the colony frequently results in instantaneous death through the rather crude leader-elimination method of "heat balling." Heat balling lends literal meaning to the saying "You're toast." Bees surround and heat the new queen to an intolerable temperature. You may wonder why— the reason is that she is an unproven outsider.

A guaranteed way for a newcomer to get "heat-balled" in an organization is to enter the organization lacking any semblance of humility and respect for the people she will lead and by giving orders prematurely based on first impressions. After all, the authority of the position alone does not ensure the commitment of followers. Beekeepers understand the tenuousness of queen-leader acceptance and try to sort out the problem. In one commonly used method, the queen is introduced in a protective cage so that the colony has time to acclimate to her presence and scent before she is released. If there is an incumbent queen in the hive, the beekeeper must remove her first since her presence will confuse the situation and make matters worse.

Virgin queens become progressively more attractive with time; therefore, keeping her alive into the age of reproductive maturity is essential. The odds that the new queen will be accepted are substantially enhanced once she mates. The colony more readily embraces a mated queen based on the expected contributions she will make to their society. The best leader is a useful leader. In this regard, by all appearances, Peter Löscher did everything right. First, he produced early successes by, for example, settling nagging, outstanding legal cases. Second, he made larger changes possible over time by preaching "evolution" versus "revolution," thereby permitting the workforce to adjust to their new leader and to have a voice in the direction of the company.

To speed up the process of acceptance, the beekeeper also can introduce an already-mated (versus virgin) queen into the hive, an experienced grande dame who will be able to contribute early in her tenure. This is comparable to the consultant, sales associate, or executive who brings customers and business with them into their new roles. They are impregnated with dollars, so to speak, and much more welcome than those who show up in the corporate entryway empty-handed.

The timing of the mated queen's introduction may also be important. Research available on the subject suggests that spring—when the population of the hive needs to be built up for the months of harvest ahead—may be the optimal time. The queen's ability to lay eggs can profoundly affect the future of the hive. This raises the intriguing question about when to hire a leader from the outside. If the wisdom of the hive has credence, the answer is, "When the circumstances are most favorable." Hiring may be tied to the seasonality of the business, new developments (e.g., patents, product releases) that portend fruitful financial conditions ahead, capital infusions, and so on. A leader from the outside world will be handicapped enough when entering a new company. Why give her another obstacle to overcome through poorly conceived timing if it can be avoided?

When change is mandatory and is unlikely to come from the incumbent management team, organizations need to be willing to go outside the team or company for the requisite talent. While the new leader should know better than to treat her new employees as clodhoppers, the hiring body could encourage her to become acquainted with her people and to assume that despite the deteriorating fortunes of the company the workforce is a vital asset. Those charged with bringing in new management might even borrow a technique from beekeeping and threaten to lower newcomers into the company in a cage if that's what it will take for them to appreciate the value of the fresh relationship and the tenuousness of their position.

Finally, employees—and bees—are often willing to accept their new leaders initially on the promise of their near-term value. However, this provisional trust will quickly fade to disbelief if they are unable to perform as expected. In the hive, these expectations are clearly measured by the number of eggs laid. The day of disbelief is doomsday for the queen. Organizational leaders are a bit more fortunate. Their deaths will be slower, but just as assured if they lose the confidence of their people.

Try not to get heat-balled.

More Pollen

Sometimes the only way to rejuvenate an organization is to hire from the outside. This is easier said than done, and deciding when to change management can be a tricky business. We all have had the experience of running into an old friend after a period of years and witnessing the effects of aging. However, if we saw our friend daily we might not notice the gradual changes. The same thing happens in companies. For example, a manager's performance may not keep pace with new technologies or market conditions. However, this does not happen overnight and so the decline in performance escapes our awareness. Leaders may have a hunch that something is amiss, but they don't completely trust their judgment and are unsure. Consequently, we accept a state of affairs that an outside observer may be inclined to reject.

Moreover, the need for a change in leadership slips in and out of focus depending on where you fix your gaze. For example, in the hive, a queen may be doing just fine laying eggs but killing the colony in other ways (e.g., passing on inherited diseases). Managers similarly may be doing well in some areas but not in others.

All told, replacing managers at any level is a tough call to make. There are no easy solutions, but it helps to know what you want and what is most important to the organization. In addition, it helps to get feedback from others. Have the courage to ask observers from the outside to validate your impressions of various attributes of your team, your organization, or your own work. If you don't have the budget or resources to hire a professional, listen to and speak with colleagues or ask a trusted peer to spend a few hours in your office, sharing his or her observations and impressions.

LESSON 19

MERGE TO MAKE GOOD ORGANIZATIONS BETTER

In nature, honeybee colonies fail. Pestilence, weather, predators, and scarcity all may be factors. Sometimes the hive is beyond the rescue of any top-notch team the queen may assemble, and without outside intervention, the hive is doomed.

As colonies falter, beekeepers can step in and facilitate a merger of hives. Since efficiency is not the issue, none of these mergers could strictly be construed as a rescue of the infirm or, comparably, as picking up bankrupt companies just because they can be acquired at bargain prices. Instead, circumstances beyond the control of the hive have afflicted the honeybees who are otherwise operationally sound. In this case, depleted ranks are the problem. In order to fulfill the tasks of the hive, they need more workers and a more robust division of labor. In essence, the hive needs to augment capabilities that are in short supply.

The basic criterion for combining hives is that the union

makes at least one of the hives more effective at what it does. If a colony, or company, were inefficient, simply adding bodies would not miraculously enhance its ability to perform. No amount of head count and "synergy" can save a clumsy company from itself. Hives in decline do not require organizational overhauls but, rather, enough workers who can be deployed in the right ways. What they need are more bees to complement their existing workforce.

This suggests that a good merger is one that enables a good company—one that is operationally sound—to do better by importing the necessary competencies. Indeed, successful mergers in companies tend to be complementary, or adjacent. The merger is a logical extension of the two businesses. The 2005 merger between Procter & Gamble and Gillette offers one good example. They have complementary customers (e.g., Gillette knows how to reach men, P&G knows how to reach women) and markets (e.g., Gillette is strong in India, where P&G wants to increase market share), and different organizational competencies of value to the other. P&G is a recognized innovator in consumer products and an able promoter of its brands. Gillette is technically sophisticated and adept at getting its products to market quickly. Hewlett-Packard's recent purchase of 3Com is another example of an acquisition that looks good on paper. The addition of 3Com's networking equipment and capabilities extends Hewlett-Packard's reach into corporate data centers and helps to protect their core server business from competitors.

As in the corporate world, combining hives is difficult because colonies are usually culturally incompatible. Each hive develops a unique identity based on genetically and environmentally variable wax comb. The chemical compounds in the wax give the bees in the hive a distinct odor that allows them to discriminate friend from foe. The bees' exposure to the nest material creates a very powerful in-group, inducing the colony's bees to reject the members of other hives. Therefore, simply putting two hives together does not suddenly make one organization, a fact most experienced leaders would agree with given that 70 percent of mergers fail in our own business world.

The stories of failed mergers are legion and research shows that cultural conflict is a frequently cited cause. The personnel from two dissimilar organizations just don't mesh. Nevertheless, bees are able to do what seems difficult for us: enlarge their circle of friends and incorporate outsiders into the in-group. This, however, requires the assistance of a neutral third party—the beekeeper. To facilitate integration, the beekeeper places comb from one hive into the receiver hive prior to introducing the bees themselves (or uses other procedures in which the scents of the two hives are gradually spread before the bees from the respective hives make physical contact). By his doing this, the receiver colony acquires a new chemical signature that reflects the odor of both colonies. This new template allows the colony to accept bees from the donor hive and the donor bees to accept the presence of bees from the receiver hive. Mutual acceptance, then, requires mutual offerings, or reciprocity.

The idea of reciprocity is a helpful reminder to those companies involved in mergers. Often when companies merge, members of one of the organizations (the stronger of the two, frequently an acquirer) feel superior to those in the other and see minimal benefit from the new association. This isn't exactly spreading the comb in both directions. A smooth merger entails recognition by the acquiring company that it is partly dependent on the acquired company for the future success of the new, combined organization. Without the presumption of mutual benefit and actual exchange of what each has to offer, even financially sound mergers will founder.

More Pollen

Whenever people from different places come together with the intent of getting along, there has to be mutual benefit for the relationship to work. Mergers that are simply extravagant mechanisms for removing costs tend to fall apart. In fact, the mega–money manager BlackRock refuses to acquire companies on these grounds, rightly claiming that cost-letting (producing savings by slashing) through the elimination of jobs and operational compression of products does not work. They want to find partners who will extend their roster of products or geographic footprint.

Good corporate unions are more like good marriages in which there is a figurative exchange of nest material to signify that the two belong together. As you invite organizations into the fold, it is preferable to assume equality and to pursue integration in a way that tends to the emotional lives of people and assures that the new combination will be personally rewarding for the organizations' members. Doing so will foster greater cooperation within, and yield better outcomes for, the new organization.

By the way, you can conceive of mergers as being on a continuum from "simple mergers" to "complex (organization-wide) mergers." Simple mergers take place when you bring a new employee into the organization. If you fail to attend to the arrival and orientation of a new hire (and the new hire correspondingly wonders if she got the start day right), then you have not done a very good job at the merger. Big groups, small groups, in-between groups, we all want the same thing—to belong—and that requires planning.

THE BEST OFFENSE IS NOT A GOOD DEFENSE— IT'S A GOOD OFFENSE

The ability of bees to tell insiders from outsiders by their unique scents plays a functional role in the hive. It enables a colony to keep out invaders who might steal their honey.

Fending off intruders in order to protect the colony's honey stores is entrusted to relatively mature bees known, appropriately, as "guards." These same bees also are old enough and physiologically equipped to forage, so when they aren't watching over the honey, they usually are in the field harvesting. This produces an inverse relationship between guarding and searching: bees that are more defensive log less flight time. On the other hand, bees that are less defensive log more flight time.

Honeybees' investment in defense ebbs and flows with conditions (the better the flow of honey, the more foragers and the fewer defenses). In general, during the months of harvest, the bees put more chips in the field than on safe-guarding honey in the hive. Regardless of the size of their stockpile, the colony tends to keep forces focused on the field. Colony growth and fitness (reproduction and the feed-ing of brood and workers) depend on the steady intake of nectar, and establishing a long-standing, rigorous pattern of defense would produce two unwelcome results. First, it would interfere with additional accumulations of nectar needed by the hive. Second, who are the honeybees defend-ing against? There are dry spells in the flower patch and, admittedly, some poaching goes on when resources are scarce, but mostly other honeybees are out on the hunt for new sources of food and building materials. Smart competi-tors are out looking for new opportunities and not hunkering down—bothering to carve up a fixed-size pie by stealing from one another. Therefore, bees will try to keep thieves out of their hive, but not at all costs.

Honeybees naturally realize that investing too much of their resources in protecting what they have denies the group a fitting chance for growth and relinquishes markets to competitors. Too much defense for too long a period is a recipe for colony failure. It seems to me that companies such as Kodak and Polaroid stayed the course for far too long and spent too much time and effort trying to safeguard what they had, thereby harming their chances to become a part of the digital age sooner. Kodak's sluggish movement into the digi-tal era is ironic, since Steve Sasson of Kodak is often credited with being the inventor of the digital camera.

LESSON 20

DIVEST TO RENEW

Successful colonies lay ample brood, add workers, and store sufficient amounts of honey to weather dry periods and harsh winters. As they thrive and grow, the bees reach an equilibrium point at which it is no longer feasible to continue increasing the size of the hive. There is a natural limit to growth. The queen can lay only so many eggs in a day (two thousand) and the hive structure can accommodate only so many bees. When the brood cells are nearly filled and no further workers are needed to tend the young and to gather water, pollen, and honey, the colony regenerates by divesting itself of a little over half of its members.

Even if the fields were lush with flowers and the honeybees could tolerate a larger population in the hive, the additions would increase worker idleness, waste, and risk. Given that a fixed number of bees care for the young, excess workers would need to be deployed in other ways and some would not be needed for anything at all. Other workers would be sent to harvest bountiful resources that would never be stored and consumed. When the day came that the flowers in the fields could no longer support the bees' burgeoning population because of shortfalls in the food supply, the colony would have to quickly eliminate workers and euphemistically call it a layoff. Therefore, for many insect colonies, including those of honeybees, the group often reaches a point in which the growth potential of two nests is greater than one.

One index of corporate success is uninterrupted growth— a rare economic event. Our honeybees, however, introduce a different point of view. To them, unremitting growth of the more-and-more variety has its limits. The colony's size can become a liability and contribute to operational inefficiencies.

A long-standing maxim in financial and corporate management holds that size is a preventative to loss as in "too big to fail." But the beehive suggests that there may be such a thing as "too big to manage." Indeed, some companies, such as W. L. Gore, a global manufacturer of polymer-based products, routinely break up business units that grow too big as a way to keep bureaucracy in check. Properly timed disposals can positively affect the financial well-being of corporations.

Bees subscribe to what we might refer to as a process of continuous renewal. The working assumption of the hive is that regular growth simply can't be maintained over time without ill effects eventually occurring. Consequently, the hive occasionally restructures. Bees restructure by shedding a significant proportion of the colony in a swarm.

The life of the hive is thus: build up, split up, start over . . .

build up, split up, start over. Many companies restructure, but there is an important difference when compared to the hive. The hive's breakup is foreshadowed and not a corporate afterthought. There is implicit acceptance of temporarily becoming smaller. There is no entrenched management team to protect sacred ground and no Wall Street to lament the shrinkage.

Management teams must weigh many factors in evaluating whether an organization will benefit from carving out a part of itself in order to create a new organization. The success of the hive as well as the experiences of successful companies provide a few guidelines for knowing when size may be impairing the leanness and agility of the corporation, and when a divestiture will create greater value. Divestiture should occur only when the new "colony" has the resources needed to have a chance at success and when the move will competitively strengthen the parent organization. In contrast, consider Verizon's sell-off of two bum businesses: their yellow pages (Idearc) and landlines (Fairpoint Communications). The financing of the deal saddled the new companies with debt and gave Verizon shareholders a controlling interest. Since consummation of the deal, both companies have raced toward insolvency. I'm sure Verizon is happy to be rid of these companies, but now they will have to prove to shareholders, particularly those left holding the bag, that they can produce greater systemic value than they gave up.

When a swarm disengages from the hive, it is not a divorce of convenience designed only to give the host hive more elbow room. The evolutionary aim is to produce a new colony that will mature and succeed. The swarm leaves with stores of honey, a disproportionate number of younger bees whose longer life spans and productivity will be instrumental to the fledgling colony, and the old queen herself—who can immediately begin building up the new hive once a site is found (the workers in the old hive will have made a new queen for themselves). Essentially, the colony provides the new cohort with adequate resources, the necessary labor, and solid leadership.

When a hive splits (or spins) off a large part of the colony, the bees are not dumping a worthless asset, but are giving the hive and the newly formed organization their best chances to remain productive. Hive divestitures create greater systemic value. The workforces of the before-and-after hive as well as the swarm have been duly considered. Both the old and the new colonies have a chance to succeed because honeybees have done their evolutionary homework by laying out the ideal overhead/asset mixes in the two organizations.

More Pollen

Organizational growth is a continual process of building up and breaking apart. No matter the nature of the group, the question is the same: "Is the team, department, unit, division, or company better off retaining a particular segment of itself or would overall value improve if the parts were divided?"

A colony, as we learned, lets loose a significant portion of itself when its size is no longer sustainable and two hives will clearly be better than one. But here's the thing: when bees produce a swarm, the swarm is provisioned and set completely free. They are on their own.

In contrast, companies often attempt to be "intrapreneurial" by creating businesses within larger businesses, but never completely severing ties. The current compensation and benefits of the employees that are used to staff the new entity are maintained, and the employees of the fledgling organization are assured a safe harbor return to the parent organization if business doesn't materialize as anticipated. The company establishes or carves out businesses but places a huge safety net underneath them. In theory, this seems like a good idea, but in practice I have never seen it work well because it doesn't motivate people to give their absolute best. If you wish to do as the bees, one way to unlock value from a pile of assets would be to create a separate, adequately stocked organization that controls its own destiny.

LESSON 21

HANDLE YOUR VALUABLES WITH CARE

You took good care of your pants growing up in my family. You cleaned them, folded them, and hung them up. You knew the colors and numbers of pairs that hung in your closet. You tried intently not to fall on a hard surface and tear a hole in a knee. I believe I have exceptional balance today due to this childhood fear of falling and ruining a perfectly good pair of pants. You also were very careful about what you bought: you only got two choices per school season. Better make sure the pants fit comfortably and were acceptably stylish since you'd be living in them for a while. Occasional growth spurts and a run of bad luck on the playground raised the harrowing and socially awkward possibility of going pantless, while raising the consternation of parents who didn't know how they would be able to afford a replacement pair. Fortunately, I had an aunt who in her cellar workshop would stitch and mend extended life into my pants until a new school season arrived. While our austere lifestyle seems old-fashioned in modern times, the belief that not everything is expendable and can easily be replenished has currency. There are relationships and things worth looking after and savoring because they are in limited supply, terribly important, and up to you to sustain. I like knowing what that feels like. It helps me to imagine what it must be like for our bees who have their pair of pants: pollen.

Pollen is king in the hive. Pollen provides the essential nutrients for the colony, with protein as its chief and most valued ingredient. Colony growth directly depends on pollen-derived protein because it is the primary source of food for developing larvae. The more pollen available, the greater the number of brood that can be nourished, and the larger the hive becomes. Thus the fitness of the hive depends upon the persistent intake of pollen.

Briefly, foraging workers (a different set from those gathering nectar) collect pollen from available plant sources and deposit their loads directly into empty, or partially full, wax comb cells that are located near the brood cells. Nurse bees consume the pollen, mix in some fine juices, and secrete a glandular substance called "brood food" or "bee bread" onto the larvae: a nonbanned, completely legit way for the nascent bees to bulk up.

Of immediate note, the bees use comb cells in a way that is conducive to efficiency. Nurse bees interact almost exclusively with newborns, so the pollen storage compartments are conveniently located adjacent to the hive's incubator cells. The proximity of the storage compartments to the incubator cells also helps foragers to discern pollen needs based on the amount of stored pollen compared with the number of brood.

The space devoted to pollen storage is relatively small, mainly because pollen isn't needed much during the winter months when brood numbers are low. The honeybees need much more room for their honey in order to get through periods of cold and inactivity. Bees, then, keep very little pollen in reserve—a modest buffer that lasts only a few days in the absence of incoming pollen. As a result, honeybees closely monitor and tightly regulate their pollen intake and supplies. Moreover, very few legs are permitted to touch the pollen: only those of the foragers who directly deposit the pollen into the wax comb cells and the nurses who ingest it and feed it to the young. Certainly, one way to maintain tight quality control is to limit the number of organisms involved and the number of exchanges in a process.

Pollen flow determines what the hive can and cannot do. Honeybees carefully budget around a homeostatic set point of pollen based on influx from the field, pollen reserves, and the amount of brood. That is, they try to maintain constancy in pollen supply while growing the hive. The colony will accommodate more brood if the store and availability of pollen in the field are more robust. If pollen quality and quantity dwindle, the colony's first response is to increase pollen production by recruiting more foragers, upping pollen loads, and reducing the time foragers take to off-load pollen and return to the field. Initial shortages, then, are met by attempts to increase pollen revenues. Conversely, they will hold back on collection if they have more pollen than they need to nourish the young.

Thus the growth of the colony is controlled: not too fast and not too slow. Honeybees do not produce brood on speculation of future unrealized pollen gains and thereby place the colony at risk of starvation. Instead, the hive will grow in tandem with its carefully measured resources. The colony manages supply and demand for incremental growth, with a three-to-five-day reserve of pollen on hand.

The budgetary discipline of the honeybees is to be applauded. First, they trade exclusively in hard currency. The bees continuously measure income and expenses in terms of real pollen. If the colony can grow, it will. If it cannot, it will not try.

If bees were witness to some of our own budget practices, they would be astounded: forget reality, assume a percent growth trajectory, and execute accordingly. I know I've been dumbfounded at some of the mindless corporate planning sessions I've witnessed where the plan and reality never clearly converge. A predetermined goal is set without forethought of how it can possibly be achieved. In contrast, I can imagine a group of bees sitting around a hexagonal table discussing their annual ambitions but couching their goals for growth around certain variables: the availability of pollen based on existing flower sources and competition, the maximum foraging force that can be deployed, the effects of seasonality, capital limits such as storage capacity, and so forth. You see, the colony naturally wants to increase its size, but it does not want to lose any bees in that pursuit. No bee is considered expendable when it is born. Enter the hive, and the expectation is that every bee will find its niche and mature into a productive adult.

Second, bees do not count every particle of pollen as

having equivalent value. Pollen with higher protein content counts far more in the hive. Bees have no direct way of assessing the protein in pollen, but they are able to use a number of indirect cues such as odor to approximate. Honeybees, then, do not fool themselves into believing that pollen is pollen is pollen. Rather, some pollen is of higher quality, and higher-quality pollen is preferred.

Companies sometimes convince themselves that dollars with equal consumption values have the same worth regardless of their source. Managers seeking to understand cash flow, or ways to support ongoing operations, should take it from the bees: an investment dollar, borrowed dollar, and operational dollar are not of equal value. You can live well on any of them for a while, but if the goal is to wed the daily activity of the company to an ability to pay, the best and surest source of funding is a dollar earned.

In spite of bees' watchfulness over pollen flows, a steady rain over several days can interfere with foraging and, therefore, deplete their reserves. Honeybees will try to forage on rainy days, but the weather can be problematic and they are not very good at it. When resources run low and intensified foraging cannot replace them, bees take a series of precautionary measures to sustain themselves. First, the queen initially halts or significantly reduces brood production. This is the equivalent of instituting a hiring freeze.

If poor conditions persist, the colony will employ more severe countermeasures. Specifically, the colony will sacrifice the youngest larvae and accelerate the capping of older larvae once the larvae have reached a secure capping stage. The threefold intent is to preserve as much pollen as possible, to protect the hive's investment in its maturing larvae, and to have a prepared adult workforce when conditions ease and foraging can start again in earnest.

The colony gives preferential treatment to those bees that are most developed and will be instrumental to the hive's recovery. Companies that have jobs with lengthy learning curves, such as Boeing and Airbus, desperately try to follow a similar prescription to that of bees by holding on to key personnel so the time needed to recover is shortened. In the industry-wide wake of the dot-com bubble, Union Pacific Corp. learned the hard way what can happen when a workforce is dramatically reduced, a recession ends, and requests for freight surge: not much. As a result, during the most recent recession, they kept the workforce prepared for the inevitable upturn by placing a subset of workers on furlough with partial wages and full benefits. Yes, this can be expensive, and without periodic training and maintenance of skills, it is not a foolproof solution. However, if the recession is not exceptionally long, furloughs can be far less costly than layoffs if you count the future costs of layoffs to the business: missed opportunities and the permanent loss of customers during the recovery period.

The colony takes aggressive steps against severe shortages of pollen only as a last resort. These steps will preserve the future of the colony, but not without adverse consequences. A generation of young will be lost and those who survive will show signs of undernourishment: lower body weights and shorter life spans. Division of labor and task scheduling are upset and many adults venture forth with bodies underequipped to efficiently harvest. After the rain stops, and the environment is again hospitable, working conditions are sufficiently disrupted that the hive will need time to return to full fitness after taking draconian measures. Similarly, it has been estimated that it takes the economy three years to fully recover from a grim recession given the time companies require to rehire and train workers and to ramp up production. Managers can do only what they can afford, but clearly retaining talent and operational capabilities during a downturn will pay off when the economy eventually returns to normalcy.

More Pollen

The lesson from the hive is to handle your most prized possessions with the utmost care and have contingencies in place in case of emergencies. And, I suppose we could add "don't panic" to the list of tips. The great economist Arthur Okun mathematically described the relationship between domestic output and unemployment, showing that unemployment predictably rises and falls with GDP (Gross Domestic Product). This relationship was reliable from the Second World War until the recent big-R recession in which more jobs have been lost than Okun would have expected. One explanation is that employers panicked and jettisoned more people than necessary, and consequently have failed to hold on to enough workers to facilitate a swifter recovery.

In the hive, pollen is preeminent. Many analysts see free cash flow as the comparable good to watch over in companies, as it's the index of the real money a company is able to generate through its operations after paying its bills and making capital expenditures. Free cash flow is the hard currency that a company uses to keep the lights on, reward shareholders, and invest in its future. Money (pollen) in, money (pollen) out sounds like a simple formula to mind but it is what keeps business—and the hive—interesting. Too little cash (pollen) is bad because it puts the organization in a precarious place. The omnipresent quest to satisfy short-term interests doesn't help because it can tempt companies to prop up reported earnings (a good thing) at the cost of depleting cash (a bad thing).

Having too much is not good either. Like the bees and pollen, leaders do not want to store too much cash since there are better ways of using it than hoarding: the bees would consider the excess wasted productivity. Besides, large stores of cash make people and companies dumb. I have an acquaintance who recently won the lottery, and after a brief period of elation, it has been all downhill. Being flush with cash can seduce you into making decisions you would not make ordinarily. Thrift (as opposed to miserliness) should not be circumstantial but exercised by managers at all times. At a minimum, managers should follow their budgets, the proxy for cash management. Perhaps if employees throughout the organization had as clear a view of the different buckets of corporate cash as the bees have of stored pollen (open-comb management), they would take greater responsibility over how money is used, treating it more like their own.

LESSON 22

DO GOOD BY DOING WELL

Without compromising their mission of survival and reproductive growth, honeybees give us plenty for which to be thankful. Indeed, the honeybee colony may well be the original sustainable enterprise. Honeybees were practicing social responsibility long before it became fashionable. In promoting growth, honeybees display a profound sensitivity to their environment. While collecting pollen, the bees pollinate the flowers, thereby replenishing the very stock they are harvesting. Pollen grains from the male part of a flower, the anther, stick to the bees. Then the bees transfer the pollen to the receptive female parts of the flower, the stigma, initiating the birthing cycle of pumpkins, cherries, cucumbers, watermelons, and hundreds of other delights. The honeybees give proper respect to the good earth whence their wealth derives.

Honeybees also are conservationists. They do not extract every drop of nectar or speck of pollen from flowers, thereby ensuring the flowers' future yield potential. In addition, bees recycle, or remanufacture, honey. If a beekeeper removes honey from a frame of honeycomb and leaves the frame in the yard, the bees will pick it clean since reusing processed goods is more energy-efficient than starting from scratch.

Honeybees' sustainable industriousness has yielded one of the most commercially successful products in history: honey. People have used honey as currency, medication, cosmetics, food, and drink. Moreover, they have used honey and bee-related products such as beeswax candles to commemorate births, baptisms, weddings, and deaths. Indeed, it was tradition for beekeepers to inform their colonies of important events, a custom known as "telling the bees." Sometimes they would leave the colony a gift such as a slice of wedding cake or, in the case of a death, drape the hive in black cloth. And, of course, every celebratory cause was sufficient reason to break out the mead, the honey-based alcoholic beverage. Adding water to honey causes it to ferment, a fact that our ancestors probably discovered very early in the history of humankind. Today mead seems a bit Arthurian, but flavorful, high-quality meads are still available. What could be finer than walking about with a mug of mead and a turkey leg?

Unbeknownst to the bees, their production of honey was fulfilling fundamental needs. They were giving those of us who celebrate, worship, and mourn a revered substance that brought us closer together. Honey was the sacred glue of a community: in fact, honey is a sensory representation *of the community* since it is a compilation of the best moments from the floral landscape. There is no other honey in the world exactly like the one from your local community. The first batch of honey from the White House, for example, was a blend of cherry trees, clover, black locust, and basswood. To generalize, the best commercial products aren't the ones that are merely consumed, but are those that are able to fulfill genuine, deep needs in those who use them, and often these needs are social in nature. The bees have it right. They have given many generations much more than honey.

We have found many other uses for the products of the honeybees' labor. Health and beauty companies have produced soothing lotions, soaps, ointments, and creams that contain beeswax and honey. In giving us pollen, honey, venom, royal jelly, and propolis, bees have provided substances with the power to heal. The medicine men of antiquity relied substantially on the wondrous products of hives for their curative powers. Apitherapies are still with us today and practitioners claim treatments for afflictions ranging from baldness to Parkinson's disease.

Briefly, scientific research shows that honey, propolis, and royal jelly contain compounds that potentially are antiviral, antibacterial, antifungal, and anti-inflammatory. For example, honey has been used as a salve for burns, a suppressant for coughs due to upper respiratory infection, and a treatment for wounds. Honey sterilizes wounds because it has properties that inhibit bacterial growth. For example, when honey and tissue meet (our tissue has a certain pH level and sodium content that starts a chemical reaction with the honey), the antibacterial agent hydrogen peroxide is formed, albeit in much lower concentrations than the bottle of hydrogen peroxide my mother kept in our medicine cabinet along with three other miracle remedies (St. Joseph's Aspirin, Vicks VapoRub, and Ben-Gay).

It is not the purpose of bees to heal our wounds, or give us light, or soften our skins, but they make all of these things possible. Bees do what they do well and we benefit. In contrast to industry in which there is often a tug-of-war between corporate and social purposes, a seamless connection exists between the colony's operations and the many benefits it bestows. The social value of the hive is firmly enveloped within its ultimate regenerative aims.

If we want vibrant communities, what we need most are successful businesses that employ ever more workers, attract other companies to town, and stimulate a healthy and prosperous retail scene. We need companies generating dollars that can keep a city's arts and educational institutions vital in a sustainable symbiotic relationship in which government, business, and the nonprofit sector all thrive. Growing businesses are the engines for prosperity, the backbone of civic engagement and beautiful streetscapes, and magnets for skilled people. We expect a lot from our businesses and sometimes they are tempted to try to do too much for too many, and lose sight of what they are in business for. The best way for a company to contribute is to be successful through responsible means.

More Pollen

The bees do good works by doing well, giving us products that make our lives, dare I say, sweeter. The bees, however, never deviate from their primary mission. They responsibly deliver their goods while sticking to what they do best—harvesting nectar and pollen. Companies, too, can do much good while at the same time remaining focused.

A company always can place money into a foundation and support causes and communities through grants and other contributions at arm's length from its operations. Additionally, some companies match the charitable contributions of employees, allow employees to volunteer time to nonprofit organizations, and place managers on nonprofit boards to lend their expertise to these organizations as well as to further their managers' personal development as future leaders. Managers also can inspire and encourage employees to be active in the community and sponsor charitable drives and events. HSBC offers a nice example of community involvement. The bank permits staff volunteers to teach schoolchildren how to manage their money. The practice raises the visibility of the bank, to be sure, but students also learn a valuable life skill.

Most of all, companies can do much good by creating high-quality products that people want and by inserting social consciousness seamlessly into their corporate strategies. For example, companies can pay farmers in developing countries a fair wage (for coffee beans, for instance), use clean energy to generate power, or use recycled goods in the manufacture of products as a fundamental way they choose to do business.

LESSON 23

TREAT YOURSELF WELL

By now, most people have heard of the mysterious colony collapse disorder (CCD) that has afflicted a sizable percentage of hives in the United States. However, you may not know about the eerie consequences of the disorder. An affected nest resembles a fully functioning hive with a queen, brood, and food reserves. Everything appears to be in order except all of the adult workers are missing—gone without a trace.

The scene is reminiscent of the haunting depictions of the silent New York City you find in sci-fi movies. Or think of a CEO sitting alone in an office tower during peak working hours: the lights are on, files are out, and communications networks are connected throughout the building. Yet the expanse of cubicles and glass-encased offices is empty, as if all of the people were instantaneously plucked from their midday routines. If, in place of this implausible scene, you picture an organizational space filled with dull workers whose every move seems weighted down with effort, we would be closer to the point I want to make regarding another version of CCD: Company Collapse Disorder.

Theories abound as to the cause of CCD in nests, with bacteria, parasites, and viruses as leading contenders—or some mixture of these and other factors. Regardless of the proximal cause, the gateway appears to be stress-related.

Like us, bees have immune systems that resist harmful invaders. Physical pain and stress can suppress their immune systems, increasing susceptibility to pathogens that bees normally can withstand, in much the same way as our immune systems can be adversely affected. We can all think of times when we have been fatigued from prolonged stretches of work or periods of mental pain and anguish. Our worn-out bodies cry out, *"No más, no más"*; unable to muster an effective response, we succumb to colds, inexplicable aches, and excessive impatience and irritability.

Bees have a naturally hard life and it seems odd that they are able to experience stress. However, they do and, as it happens, the stress is often man-made. Feral populations of bees have declined over the years partly to make room for our progressive incursions into the wilderness. Nonetheless, our concentrated fields of almonds, avocados, and blueberries require pollination to reproduce and, so, we still need bees—lots of them. Consequently, many thousands of hives are loaded on trucks and transported thousands of miles to sites needing the bees' services.

This year-round migratory labor takes a toll on bees for two reasons. First, they frequently are moved during times of the year when they are accustomed to rest, such as the month of February. Like our sports stars, bees need a recuperative period: an off-season to gather one's strength for what lies ahead. Second, because of their busy schedule, the bees are not able to gather, store, and consume their customary foods. Their diet instead consists of a high-fructose syrup mix that is like drinking soda for every meal (plus, the fructose corn syrup produces a toxic substance—hydroxymethylfural—when heated). The nutritional value of a bees' diet is found in the protein, minerals, and vitamins of pollen, not in sweets.

So there you have it: hard work, crazy hours, and poor diet. Sound familiar? No wonder, then, that mobile hives have higher incidences of bacteria, fungi, viruses, and para-sites than are found in stationary colonies. In addition to the likely spread of disease through contact among bees of different colonies in the field (much like what happens to us on a crowded airplane), the physical movement of hives is stressful.

Companies can do many things to alleviate the stresses of the workplace. They can sponsor health-related clinics and annual checkups, promote balanced diets in the cafe-teria, replace Friday's Danish with fruit platters, make the staircases more comfortable and inviting, encourage a sen-sible work-life balance, emphasize good hygiene, and force employees to take a real vacation. Quite a few fine compa-nies do all of these things. These companies understand that the investments in its people will pay off in the form of bet-ter health and fewer absences. In addition, they understand that high performance requires stamina and mental acuity, and that concentrated effort is possible only if our bodies allow it. Thus, we need to take good care of ourselves—if not to work smarter and more productively, then for a longer, happier life.

Even if we are able to repel the detrimental effects of stress and preserve our physical fitness and sanity, acts designed to reduce stress require effort and affect performance. Before our bodies yield to stress, we try to temper its effects. Bees, for example, engage in a number of antiseptic behaviors such as grooming and cleaning as a means to rid the colony of pests. Similarly, we try to manage stressors through either proactive coping strategies or attitudinal adjustments. Regardless of the species of animal or particular form an effective response may take, all responses require attention and the expenditure of energy. For bees and for us there are costs to these defenses.

Stress in the hive or the corporation imposes social costs with a subsequent loss in overall productivity. Some of those costs can be insidious. Recent research shows that persistent stress leads to a virulent form of habit formation: under stress, we tend to do the same things over and over again even when the actions we take get us nowhere. Therefore, one of the best things a company can do is to create environments that filter out unnecessary stresses. For example, employees' anxieties can be alleviated through frequent communications about the status and direction of the company and by giving employees greater control over critical events that directly affect them in order to take evasive actions when necessary. People who are cast as potent are less stressed and more effective actors.

The invariable end to unyielding stressors is the depletion of one's reserves and exhaustion. The result is Company Col-

TREAT YOURSELF WELL ••• 165

lapse Disorder, or, as it is sometimes called, "disappearing disease." This seems an appropriate term for a workforce that is on its way out and has all but vanished on the job.

More Pollen

Fatigue, inactivity, and poor diet impose heavy individual and social costs on organizational performance—so take care of your health. Do not end up like the bees that have been succumbing to what appears to be, at least in part, a stress-related affliction.

Organizations can promote health in many ways. First, your organization will be less stressful if you follow the many lessons about good organizational design and leadership outlined in this book.

Second, organizations can encourage employees to stay fit, physically and mentally. Most companies realize that workplaces that support healthy lifestyles are good for employees and good for business. Some corporate health-related facilities are extensive; for example, the technology company SAS has running and bike trails on their North Carolina campus. Unilever recently began a pilot program that is more representative of what avant-garde companies are doing. That program, "Fit Business," provides better food choices at the cafeteria, prompts increased physical activity, and helps employees to monitor and manage key indicators of health (e.g., blood pressure). One company, Lundberg Family Farms, started a vegetable garden as a part of the company's wellness program. Some companies also sponsor special clinics in a variety of health-promotion areas, including smoking cessation programs, relaxation training, and instruction on coping skills strategies.

Sometimes employees fail to take advantage of these programs or the time to pursue activities outside of work. Therefore, an important third thing you can do is give employees permission to have a modicum of balance in their lives by, for example, communicating that unproductive "face time" into the early evening is not as important as achieving results during a reasonable workweek. A culture of staying late ostensibly to prove one's value is an unnecessary outlay of time and energy. Of course, it ultimately is up to you to take advantage of your organization's health-related offerings.

LESSON 24

CREATE BEAUTIFUL, FUNCTIONAL SPACES

The ancient Greek mathematicians realized that only three regular polygons could tile a flat surface without leaving gaps: equilateral triangles, squares, and regular hexagons. Two thousand years later, mathematician Thomas C. Hales, of the University of Michigan, solved the Honeycomb Conjecture, which showed that the hexagonal shape of the bees' honeycomb is truly the best shape to divide a surface. His proof demonstrated that the hexagon provides the greatest allowance for storage and simultaneously minimizes the total perimeter of the shapes (i.e., it uses the least amount of material). The honeybee, nature's little designer, has created an architectural masterpiece.

The hexagonal mesh of the comb also has the additional benefit of being remarkably sturdy despite having walls that only are 0.003 inch thick. One pound of beeswax is able to support twenty pounds of honey. This durable construction inspired the minimalist design of the "Water Cube," the remarkable site of the aquatic competitions during the 2008

Summer Olympic Games in Beijing. Based on the work of physicists Denis Weaire and Robert Phelan, the "Cube" consists of four thousand specially manufactured hexagonal panels ("bubbles") that support a structure 580 feet long and 100 feet high.

Honeybees form cylindrical shapes on a vertical surface using wax secretions from eight epidermal glands. The beeswax consists of over eighty organic compounds, including hydrocarbons, wax esters, and fatty acids. Bees use gravity to orient themselves, so the honeycomb runs up and down as opposed to sitting horizontally. The bees heat the wax to make it easier for them to mold and work into what will become the bees' future storage and birthing chambers. As the wax cylinders soften and touch one another, their edges form flat surfaces at points of contact, like two soap bubbles whose sides stretch and elongate as they come together. One bubble surrounded by six bubbles produces a hexagon, and on and on it goes, with the wax cooling in the familiar textbook honeycomb pattern. What's more, the bees dig out and slant the cell chambers upward (at consistent 120-degree angles) in order to prevent spillage. It is easy to see how great mathematicians and artists found beauty in certain geometric forms, and the honeycomb—with its hints of the harmonious and divine—was no exception.

But how does this apply to the business world? A common belief among practitioners of organizational design is that form follows function. The idea is to organize physical structures according to the purposes of the space rather than based on whim, convention, or convenience. Unfortunately, we often make the mistake of associating "functional" with "bland" and conclude that which is useful cannot also be interesting. Why else do so many offices look the way they do? And, yet, the honeycomb suggests otherwise. There is nothing more functional; it is a shelter, workspace, nursery, storage area, and communications network. Its design, nevertheless, is a work of art, proof that we needn't make usable spaces boring. At the very least, I would rather sit in a "hexicle" that is representative of the tenacious worker bee than in a cubicle that employees tend to associate with a pen for dumb livestock. When Frank Lloyd Wright built the bee-inspired Hanna House in 1937, its owner, Jean Hanna, reportedly remarked, "To live here in its honeycombed space, is to live imaginatively." Many other architects, such as Gaudí, Taut, Steiner, Van der Rohe, Le Corbusier, and Ito, have similarly fulfilled their missions by finding inspiration in the patterns and shapes of the hive.

Yes, form should follow function, but the form should also help us to feel more connected to our place of work and alive.

More Pollen

Over the centuries, we have derived pleasure from the heavenly hexagonal design of the comb. Bees have inspired and fueled our imaginations, and shown us that place matters.

Different physical environments elicit different responses. Specifically, the space and the associated norms that it reflects and shapes suggest ways we should behave. Enter a church, mosque, or synagogue and the expectation is to show reverence, a different sort of appreciative response than that engendered by a stroll into a sports stadium. Companies have the opportunity to communicate what they value by constructing distinctive workspaces. They can convey class and elegance through upscale materials; playfulness and creativity through employee art and sundry games scattered about; continuity and purpose through display of historical objects; seriousness and intensity through the iron gaze of oil portraits hung against stark wood paneling; curiosity and experimentation through manufacturing puzzles openly set up for passersby to solve; and so forth. The options are plentiful—constrained only by your imagination and boldness to deviate from the traditional decor.

MISTAKES HAPPEN—MAKE SURE YOU MAKE THE RIGHT ONES

The aesthetics of the honeycomb is subject to certain constraints, primarily the expenditure of energy. The design itself is economical. However, the bees still face a resource allocation dilemma concerning when and how much honeycomb to build. Bees incur heavy costs when building comb. The wax is produced from the sugars of stored honey and is molded through thermoregulation. The use of the honey reserves and expenditure of energy is significant. Therefore, building too much comb too soon will deplete honey stores, occupy workers who otherwise could be more productively used on other tasks, and threaten the viability of the hive. On the other hand, doing too little too late will rob bees of their vital foodstuff in the future as they won't have the requisite storage space for their honey.

This is a familiar allocation problem in business since it is germane to a number of issues ranging from space planning to the production and sale of product: produce too much and it sits on a shelf; produce too little and people will buy another company's goods, or none at all, creating a highly tangible opportunity cost.

Honeybees construct comb in pulses, contingent on two related conditions: nectar flow and the proportion of the cells that are filled with honey. It has been speculated—and it makes sense—that the bees have a mobile threshold level, or criterion, for building. When very little nectar is available in the field, the threshold for space is high, i.e., the fuller the comb has to be for work to commence. Similarly, if the nectar is falling like manna from heaven, then the bees will accept a lower criterion for comb building, i.e., the bees tolerate more open space to begin comb construction.

This sliding criterion protects against the worst-case fitness scenarios. The greatest toll on colony health would occur if the colony built too much comb when nectar wasn't available or failed to build when it was. In the former case, the bees are foolishly using up their precious resources (honey is the raw material for comb) at a time when the resources will be difficult to replenish. In the latter case, they will have squandered an opportunity to better secure their future.

If a honeybee is going to make a mistake, the natural preference is to overbuild when the nectar is flowing in and underbuild when nectar is sparse. The variable criterion regarding the availability of space biases decisions in these directions. A lowered space criterion when nectar is readily available will result in a greater likelihood of building. A raised criterion when nectar is not available will depress building. Nevertheless, having too much space when times are good and too little when times are bad are not poor positions to be in.

Capacity decisions in business frequently aren't this simple since the "honey" itself comes and goes. When a car manufacturer builds a plant based on demand and consumers then abruptly stop spending, in essence, the comb is still there but the honey reserves have been reduced. That puts companies such has Toyota and Nissan in a position that the bees try to avoid: too much capacity (comb) given the slow flow of consumers (nectar). The decisions that the companies subsequently face, however, have parallels to the hive. Do you dismantle the comb as Toyota did when it closed a major production facility—closing the gap between utilization and demand—or do you keep plants open and run at 44 percent capacity as Nissan has elected to do? The answer partially depends on what the companies expect will happen in the marketplace and the type of error they prefer to make. Toyota risks a quick market turnaround and an insufficient response in fulfilling demand—not enough comb to store the honey. Toyota's decision makes sense if the market remains flat or slow moving. On the other hand, Nissan risks squandering its facility-related costs if consumers return to showrooms at a crawl. Nissan's decision would make sense if market demand were to surge.

Admittedly, it is impossible to avoid these sorts of dilemmas in business, but we can take the bees' general principal to heart in any event and work toward solutions that accommodate it: never, ever build a Field of Dreams. It's too risky. Build only what you think you will need based on the facts of the situation. Had debt-strained Dubai only known. . . .

LESSON 25

GIVE PEOPLE SOMETHING TO CARE ABOUT

In spite of their short, intense lives, honeybees have it easy in at least one way: they do not have to contend with themselves to get things done. They do not get in their own or one another's way. They are not distracted by the latest office intrigue or happenings at home; they do not have to put up with strange bosses or coworkers; and they need not huddle in endless meetings or get sidetracked by the latest corporate fad. All they have to do is their work, which they do very well. I hope that you now realize that the work they do is much more complicated and involves greater discretion to perform than you may have previously thought. At any rate, we should not downplay the bees' achievements simply because they have managed to avoid many of our pitfalls. We could avoid them well enough if we tried hard enough.

We, too, could have a colony's single-mindedness, the equivalent of a cause worth flying for. Every day the bees are on a lifesaving mission on behalf of the hive and future generations. Propelled by impulse, for eons honeybees have cultivated a social life larger than the aggregated efforts of solitary bees, honing their joint survival skills in passage. Does it really matter if nature divines their purpose and we create ours? Hive or business, a group can cut through a lot of clutter if bound together by a common goal and grand purpose in which it tries to accomplish something special.

When our bees emerge from their winter retreat in the spring, as they did once again this year, I feel a range of emotions. I feel a combination of joy and relief that our little friends have once again outlasted the elements. I also feel blessed, as if I have been invited to an exclusive gathering or a timeless rite. It is enough to put me back to work with the hive. I will not work as hard as the bees, but I will do my best to do my part. Some of the honey will be a nice reward, but the best gift the bees give a worker like me is something to care about.

More Pollen

This final lesson is not about the bees per se, but about you. Throughout life, you will discover—if you haven't already—that you are best at doing what you love most. In the most extreme cases, people are able to convert their hobbies into moneymaking ventures, as when Kate Rothacker recently turned scrapbooking into Cozy Crop House, a company that offers affordable scrapbooking retreats. We are not all so lucky but, thankfully, a large proportion of us find our way eventually. Companies can go a long way to make work more enjoyable and meaningful for their employees, but they cannot do it all. They cannot dictate what you should be passionate about and they cannot save you from false ambitions, the confining expectations of others, or negative thinking.

All I can say is that you always have a choice and that it will help you in your journey to travel with the twin virtues of compassion and humility—attributes that transform those who are less endowed into superheroes—if one is to believe fairy tales. In the Grimms' "Queen Bee," for example, it is the youngest of three brothers who demonstrates his high character by loving and defending the small, helpless creatures of Earth—including saving a bee colony from his wayward brothers, who intend to get at the bees' honey by burning down the tree in which they live—and proves worthy of assistance when he needs it most. Later, as the brothers come upon an enchanted kingdom, the older boys are turned into stone as their attempts to break a spell upon the kingdom fail. The youngest brother, portrayed as the simpleton in the story, however, succeeds because others are willing to help him, particularly those he helped in the past. Faced with the almost impossible task of choosing which, among three nearly identical princesses, is the youngest, the Queen of the Bees comes to his aid. The only clue the brother is given is that the youngest princess tasted honey before falling into a trancelike sleep. The Queen lands on her lips to indicate to the brother which of the three women to choose. He does, the spell is broken, boy gets girl, inherits kingdom, and lives happily ever after.

CONCLUSION

In this book, we have discussed several lessons about leadership derived from our understanding of the social structures of the honeybee hive. One way to think about the lessons is that they reflect core dilemmas that the bees encounter and must resolve. Specifically, honeybees appear to contend with four competing demands:

1. Short-term versus long-term gains
2. Individuality versus community
3. Stability versus flexibility
4. Similarity versus change

In managing these, the bees are not simply looking for a fixed equilibrium point in which each side of a dilemma is weighted the same. They emphasize one or the other as needed. A situation may call for a little more of this and a little less of that. Over time, behavioral patterns emerge

that reveal the bees' true leanings, such as their orientation toward the longer term.

Colonies do a good job of managing the tensions of opposing forces, but as I review each dilemma as it applies to the hive, consider the difficulties executives may have in trying to reconcile these dilemmas in their respective companies. It isn't easy.

Short-term Versus Long-term Gains

The macro-level principle that provides the context for all that bees do is their long-term focus and moderation of risk. They never take their five eyes off their distal aims or put themselves in an all-or-none position in which the life of the hive is placed in jeopardy. The honeybees continually monitor the intake of nectar and pollen to stay vital. Short-term decisions are based on their implications for the long term. Bees do not neglect the short term, but they never surrender allegiance to future growth and survival.

In the corporate world, it takes a great deal of self-restraint to avoid being captive to the immediate circumstances and rewards. If personal temptation does not get ahold of you, there is still a good chance that social pressures will. For example, those bankers who refrained from making risky loans often had to justify their actions to puzzled directors (and other interested onlookers) who watched as their banks seemingly squandered opportunities that other banks were enjoying. Herds can be very persuasive when they are headed straight for you. Today, the banks that were able to resist the go-go years of "innovative" mortgage lending are buying and growing on the cheap.

BEE ADVISED

Position yourself in the short term in a way that gives you desirable options and sound capabilities in the long term. Maintain your organization's preparedness through fiscal responsibility and strategic farsightedness. Move forward with care, taking actions that ensure that the organization remains fit for future undertakings.

Individuality Versus Community

Colonies have many thousands of workers who act according to information gathered and conveyed by others and through their own observations. Only rarely, however, do bees use their discretion for selfish purposes. Rather, almost everything the honeybee does is for the good of the colony, and almost everything done for the good of the colony is done by the worker bee. A "worker bee" is by no means a negative description of someone—or shouldn't be. Rather than being unimportant, worker bees are the quintessence of the colony. Their work may be likened to a well-choreographed dance troupe whose steps are carefully coordinated in order to make the overall production a success.

Performance is critical in the hive, and honeybees are rather tough and unsentimental about cutting loose members whose contributions have become suspect. However, they also are able to maintain unity within the hive, in part through high interdependence of tasks, uniform dispersal of the queen's commands, excellent communication networks, and enforcement of cooperation. The success of the colony depends on individuals working in harmony. The task of companies is to integrate individuals in ways that permit individual performances to stand out but that still cohere to the results of the group.

BEE ADVISED

Attend to employees' irrepressible needs for personal growth, noting their unique contributions while keeping them situated within a cooperative enterprise. That is, ensure that individuals succeed within the broader framework of the company's mission.

Stability Versus Flexibility

The ability to adapt is a precondition for organizational longevity. Throughout this book, we have discovered methods that honeybees use to vary their behavior, not the least of which is their acute sensitivity to environmental changes, embrace of diversity, openness to inputs from the field, and talent for coordination. Most important, they have demonstrated an ability to make quick adjustments based on feedback from the field.

A fine line exists between an organization that is too policy-constrained to be responsive and one that permits too much freedom to generate focused activity. The bees instruct that discipline does not necessarily imply confinement, and agility does not necessarily imply lack of structure.

BEE ADVISED

Develop standards, hire and deploy a diverse, intellectually engaged workforce, and establish organizational cadences that, taken together, promote orderliness and balance without choking out novelty and innovation.

Similarity Versus Change

Not everything in the hive involves change. In fact, quite a lot of what bees do is repetitious. Bees have their ways of doing things, and they perform their chores admirably and with great regularity. While we have become accustomed to thinking that "the only constant is change," in actuality, companies make an awful lot of progress by sticking with what they have—quality leadership, for example—and relying on the fundamentals of sound execution. Not everything can be new and exciting, although, as was noted, bees have an enviable program of development and advancement in place that offers job variety and skill building, and they are actively engaged in ongoing discovery. More to the point, innovation and invention must be supported by hard work and persistence.

Furthermore, the idea of change often has an upward thrust, but as the bees instruct, growth also is accomplished through shrinkage and regeneration. Change is not always "more" or "bigger." As an example, Youngstown (Ohio), a rust-belt city with many abandoned buildings, decided to reduce its size in order to grow. Beginning in the mid-1970s, the steel mills along the Mahoning River began to close. For many years, the city tried vainly to restore its former size just to see itself waste away further. Youngstown's mayor and town planners finally decided to shrink the city deliberately by clearing away decrepit buildings in order to create more green space, preserve property values, and make the city more livable for families. The government of Youngstown would be the first to admit that one of its greatest challenges was to acknowledge that the best way to grow was to first become smaller. This change in outlook may be paying off, as *Entrepreneur* magazine in 2009 named Youngstown one of the ten best cities in which to start a business.

BEE ADVISED

Review the factors that may sustain the status quo through their influence (e.g., attitudinal inertia, stodgy methods and procedures, tentative decision making), and take actions that rejuvenate the company and keep it receptive to changes in the environment—both current and anticipated—in order to make quick, effective responses.

Leadership is like working with a Rubik's Cube, trying to find the proper position and alignments among aspects of companies that are not inherently consistent. It involves the skillful management of oppositional forces and dilemmas for which there are no ready answers. The Cube is studiously handled and, as such, is always in motion, refined by intelligence and trial and error. Honeybees have given us a sampling of the twists and turns they make in their struggles. What they have done has worked for them.

ACKNOWLEDGMENTS

I am indebted to many people for graciously reading and commenting on this manuscript during various phases of its development. I want to thank above all else my wife, Stephanie, who forsook her own writing on evenings and weekends to review several iterations of the manuscript. Moreover, even though I use her as a foil once or twice in the book, being the good sport she is, she never once insisted that I strike those sections. She easily could have pushed for coauthor but selflessly relinquished above-the-line credit. My son, Ryan, added his observations to the material and was a patient listener as I periodically discussed ideas with him. My daughter, Kathryn, read and edited a late version of this book and proved that the child has surpassed the parent. Her comments were invaluable. As the family became increasingly preoccupied with this work, it was my mother-in-law, Peggy Samples, who kept the household running and the place comfortable. If you ever get a mother-in-law, I suggest you get one like Peggy.

My dear friend writer Susan Neitlich helped to give shape to the story in its formative stages and pointed me in the right direction early on. Two of the great international experts on bees, Madeleine Beekman and Thomas Seeley, kindly agreed to read through the manuscript to make sure I wasn't overstating or misstating what bees really do. They each made many helpful, substantive edits and suggestions; naturally, if there are errors in my reporting, they are attributable to me and me alone.

Experienced and worldly executives Robert Bremner, Michael Critelli, and Roxanne Quimby helped me to get the right balance between the bee and business worlds by commenting on where I could use a little more or a little less connection between the two domains, where elaboration on particular issues was essential, and where I needed to be more concrete. I am further indebted to Roxanne Quimby for her kind words and encouragement throughout this project. I cannot think of anyone more fitting to comment on this book than the person who has successfully straddled the executive suite and the beehive as an outstanding entrepreneur who started a bee-products company!

Robert Cole applied his unique and discerning outlook as a financial executive to the manuscript and made it better through his insights. Joseph Guaraccia, MD, the head of a neurology practice by day and lover of literature by night, highlighted places in the text where the management of groups and the behavior of colonies most clearly intersect based on his experiences, and graciously took the time to edit sections of the work. I also am indebted to Suchitra Krishnan-Sarin for her careful reading of the manuscript and for calling out ideas in the book that required clarification or greater elaboration and emphasis.

In my life as an editor, I have had occasion to meet many wonderful people, and one of the best of the best is Herb Schaffner. Through his media company, Schaffner Media Partners, Herb carefully reviewed the text and provided invaluable feedback. I also am deeply appreciative of those who believed in this book and made it a reality: my agent, Susan Ginsburg, and the good folks at Portfolio, especially Adrian Zackheim and Adrienne Schultz.

Finally, I would like to thank Lindsey Voskowsky for creation of the book's graphics and Marlene Donahue and Mary Schnabel for keeping me organized and for ably transcribing my written words that, in these modern times, I still produce in longhand—but not by candlelight.

LESSON 1: Protect the Future

The best way to ensure that there will be a short term is to focus on the long term.

LESSON 2: Keep Energy Levels Up

Preserve the future ability of the company to perform.

LESSON 3: Let Merit Be Your Guide

Concentrate on employees' ability and performance versus relationship ties and cronyism.

LESSON 4: Promote Community, Sanction Self-interest

Cooperation is not a naturally occurring phenomenon—unified action requires deliberate, ongoing attention.

LESSON 5: Distribute Authority

Those closest to the information should make the decision.

LESSON 6: Make Good Enough Decisions

Few decisions can be made with certainty but, with diligence, all decisions can be made soundly and carry the authority of action.

LESSON 7: Order and Innovate Through Fuzzy Constants

Meaningful progress and creativity requires fixed points of reference and allowance for "optimal error."

LESSON 8: Stay in Touch

Use measurement and feedback to closely monitor the market environment and the current state of the organization, and to react accordingly.

LESSON 9: Keep It Simple

The best actions often are the most parsimonious, involving clear, direct, and uncomplicated communications and actions.

LESSON 10: Find Your Zeitgebers

Develop organizational rhythms that tune organizational action to market opportunities.

LESSON 11: Design "Flexigid" Systems

Organizational responsiveness is best fulfilled by staffing plans and deployments that can be stretched and adapted as conditions warrant.

LESSON 12: Preserve a Positive Workplace

Establish a healthy work milieu through active promotion and by clearing out "diseased" elements from the organization.

LESSON 13: Keep Your Balance

Reliable and steady organizational activity depends on the smart merger of diverse talents and ideas.

LESSON 14: Discover and Use the Specialized Talents of Your Employees

Allocate people's talents, time, and efforts to well-designed activities for which they are best suited.

LESSON 15: Develop Your Team

Improve organizational performance by implementing intelligent and honest programs for individual growth and advancement.

LESSON 16: Outcompete by Outfinessing Rivals

Collective speed and effectiveness depend on the constant intake and use of data.

LESSON 17: Prepare for Leadership Changes

Prevent costly voids in leadership by planning for successors well in advance of the obvious need.

LESSON 18: Bring in New Blood for New Life

Sometimes the only way to rejuvenate an organization is to hire from the outside.

LESSON 19: Merge to Make Good Organizations Better

Concentrate on combining companies where there is obvious mutual benefit.

LESSON 20: Divest to Renew

Organizational growth is an ongoing, up-and-down process of building up and breaking apart.

LESSON 21: Handle Your Valuables with Care

Handle your most prized possessions carefully—and have procedures in place in case of emergencies.

LESSON 22: Do Good by Doing Well

Organizations can achieve their greatest social good by responsibly pursuing their central purposes.

LESSON 23: Treat Yourself Well

Fatigue, inactivity, and poor diet impose heavy individual and social costs on organizational performance—take care of yourself.

LESSON 24: Create Beautiful, Functional Spaces

Design workplaces that inspire and fuel imagination.

LESSON 25: Give People Something to Care About

Make it psychologically worth showing up for work.

NOTES

Foreword

xiv. L. L. Langstroth, the man who: L. L. Langstroth, *Langstroth's Hive and the Honey-Bee* (Mineola, N.Y.: Dover Publications, 2004).

Introduction

7. When he is later brought back: A. C. Doyle, *His Last Bow: A Reminiscence of Sherlock Holmes* (New York: George H. Doran Co., 1917), p. 302.

Lesson 1: Protect the Future

15. Minimally, these companies do: *Wall Street Journal*, April 6, 2009, p. A1.

Lesson 2: Keep Energy Levels Up

20. The resulting pilot fatigue: *Wall Street Journal*, May 14, 2009, p. A3.

Lesson 3: Let Merit Be Your Guide

27. On the other hand, we can appreciate: *Fortune*, April 27, 2009, p. 80.

Lesson 5: Distribute Authority

36. In contrast, Railroad Associates Corp.: *Wall Street Journal*, September 28, 2009, p. R5.

Lesson 6: Make Good Enough Decisions

44. In the words of Eli Lilly's: *Financial Times*, April 6, 2009, p. 10.

Lesson 7: Order and Innovate Through Fuzzy Constants

55. It used to be that baristas: *BusinessWeek*, August 17, 2009, p. 28.

Lesson 8: Stay in Touch

59. A. G. Lafley, the former CEO of Procter & Gamble: *Wall Street Journal*, March 23, 2009, p. B6.
63. At the end of the month: *Economist*, February 28, 2009, p. 67.

Lesson 9: Keep It Simple

66. the unwilling picked from the unfit: *New York Times*, April 4, 1960.

66. I recently read about a product: *Pittsburgh Post-Gazette*, July 12, 2009, p. B2.

70. Then they set about to streamline: *Fortune*, August 31, 2009, p. 82.

Lesson 11: Design "Flexigid" Systems

83. . . . as steelmaker Nucor recently did: *BusinessWeek*, March 9, 2009, p. 55.

84. In fact, futurist Peter Schwartz: *Wired*, August 2009, p. 108.

Lesson 13: Keep Your Balance

92. For example, the Danish enzyme: *Wall Street Journal*, June 22, 2009, p. R4.

Lesson 16: Outcompete by Outfinessing Rivals

111. Consider the way Zara: *Wall Street Journal*, March 26, 2009, p. B1.

117. Elting Morison (historian and founder . . . : Elting E. Morison, *Men, Machines, and Modern Times* (Cambridge, Mass.: MIT Press, 1966), pp. 17–44.

Lesson 17: Prepare for Leadership Changes

121. When CEO Kenneth Lewis: *Wall Street Journal*, November 20, 2009, p. B3.

122. In contrast to honeybees' conscientiousness: *BusinessWeek*, May 11, 2009, p. 30.

123. In fact, Apple's share prices: *Fortune*, February 2, 2009, p. 96.

123. Although former CEO Douglas Daft: *Fortune*, May 31, 2004, p. 84.

127. The stinging abuse sometimes inflicted: Lauren Weisberger, *The Devil Wears Prada* (New York: Doubleday, 2003); 20th Century Fox, 2006.

127. . . . and cataloged by author Susan Shapiro Barash: Susan Shapiro Barash, *Tripping the Prom Queen* (New York: St. Martin's Press, 2006).

128. Indeed, there is some survey evidence: *New York Times*, May 10, 2009, p. BU1.

128. Yet women make up around 50 percent: *Wall Street Journal*, January 21, 2009, p. B11; *Financial Times*, April 30, 2009, p. 10.

Lesson 18: Bring in New Blood for New Life

131. Newly hired outside executives: *Harvard Business Review*, June 2007, p. 26.

132. Think how Peter Löscher: *Financial Times*, November 9, 2009, p. B1.

Lesson 19: Merge to Make Good Organizations Better

138. Gillette is technically sophisticated: *Economist*, August 11, 2007, p. 61.

138. The addition of 3Com's: *New York Times*, November 12, 2009, p. B1.

139. . . . 70 percent of mergers fail: *Chief Executive*, April/May 2007, p. 44.

140. They want to find partners: *Fortune*, August 11, 2009, p. 102.

Lesson 20: Divest to Renew

144. Indeed, some companies, such as W. L. Gore: *Financial Times*, December 2, 2008, p. 10.

145. The financing of the deal: *Wall Street Journal*, August 11, p. C1.

Lesson 21: Handle Your Valuables with Care

153. As a result, during the most recent: *Wall Street Journal*, May 18, 2009, p. B1.

154. Similarly, it has been estimated: *New York Times*, April 7, 2009, p. B1.

154. One explanation is that employers panicked: *New York Times Magazine*, July 26, 2009, p. 11.

Lesson 22: Do Good by Doing Well

160. The bank permits staff volunteers: *Financial Times*, July 21, 2009, p. 10.

Lesson 23: Treat Yourself Well

164. Recent research shows that persistent: *New York Times*, August 18, 2009, p. D2.

165. One company, Lundberg Family Farms: *Wall Street Journal*, August 18, 2009, p. B5.

Lesson 24: Create Beautiful, Functional Spaces

172. Do you dismantle: *BusinessWeek*, November 2, 2009, p. 34.

Conclusion

182. The government of Youngstown: *Economist*, October 10, 2009, p. 37.

BIBLIOGRAPHY

Books

Bishop, H. (2005). *Robbing the bees: A biography of honey*. New York: Free Press.

Brackney, S. (2009). *Plan bee: Everything you ever wanted to know about the hardest-working creatures on the planet*. New York: Penguin.

Ellis, H. (2004). *Sweetness and light: The mysterious history of the honeybee*. New York: Harmony Books.

Gould, J. L., and Gould, C. G. (1994). *The animal mind*. New York: Scientific American Library.

Horn, T. (2005). *Bees in America: How the honey bee shaped a nation*. Lexington: The University of Kentucky Press.

Langstroth, L. L. (2004). *Langstroth's hive and the honey-bee*. Mineola, N.Y.: Dover Publications.

Lindauer, M. (1961). *Communication among social bees.* Cambridge, Mass.: Harvard University Press.

Longwood, W. (1985). *The queen must die and other affairs of bees and men.* New York: W. W. Norton.

Maeterlinck, M. (2006). *The life of the bee.* Mineola, N.Y.: Dover Publications.

Michener, C. D. (1984). *The social behavior of the bees.* Cambridge, Mass.: Belknap Press.

Ransome, H. M. (2004). *The sacred bee in ancient times and folklore.* Mineola, N.Y.: Dover Publications.

Readicker-Henderson, E. (2009). *The short history of the honey bee: Humans, flowers, and bees in the eternal chase for honey.* Portland, Ore.: Timber Press.

Samataro, D., and Avitable, A. (1998). *The beekeeper's handbook.* Ithaca, N.Y.: Cornell University Press.

Seeley, T. D. (1995). *The wisdom of the hive: The social physiology of honey bee colonies.* Cambridge, Mass.: Harvard University Press.

Tautz, J. (2008). *The buzz about bees: Biology of a superorganism.* Berlin: Springer-Verlag.

Von Frisch, K., and Seeley, T. D. (1993). *The dance language and orientation of bees.* Cambridge, Mass.: Belknap Press.

Wilson, B. (2004). *The hive: The story of the honeybee and us.* London: John Murray Publishers.

Winston, M. L. (1987). *The biology of the honey bee.* Cambridge, Mass.: Harvard University Press.

Articles

Anderson, C., and Ratnieks, F.L.W. (1999). "Worker allocation in insect societies: Coordination of nectar foragers and nectar receivers in honey bee colonies." *Behavioral Ecology and Sociobiology* 46, 73–81.

Baird, E., Srinivasan, M. V., Zhang, S., and Cowling, A. (2005). "Visual control of flight speed in honeybees." *Journal of Experimental Biology* 208, 3895–3905.

Barron, A. B., Oldroyd, B. P., and Ratnieks, F.L.W. (2001). "Worker reproduction in honey-bees and the anarchic syndrome: A review." *Behavioral Ecology and Sociobiology* 50, 199–208.

Beekman, M. (2004). "Is her majesty home?" *Trends in Ecology and Evolution* 19, 505–506.

Beekman, M., Fathke, R. L., and Seeley, T. D. (2006). "How does an informed minority of scouts guide a honeybee swarm as it flies to a new home?" *Animal Behaviour* 71, 161–171.

Beekman, M., Gilchrist, A. L., Duncan, M., and Sumpter, J. T. (2007). "What makes a honeybee scout?" *Behavioral Ecology and Sociobiology* 61, 985–995.

Beekman, M., and Lew, J. B. (2008). "Foraging in honeybees—when does it pay to dance?" *Behavioral Ecology* 19, 255–262.

Beekman, M., Oldroyd, B. P., and Myerscough, M. (2003). "Sticking to their choice—honey bee subfamilies abandon declining food sources at a slow but uniform rate." *Ecological Entomology* 28, 233–238.

Biesmeijer, J. C., and deVries, H. (2001). "Exploration and exploitation of food sources by social insect colonies: A revision of the scout-recruit concept." *Behavioral Ecology and Sociobiology* 49, 89–99.

Bogdanov, S., Jurendic, T., Sieber, R., and Gallmann, P. (2008). "Honey for nutrition and health: A review." *Journal of the American College of Nutrition* 27, 677–689.

Breed, M. D., Diaz, P. H., and Lucero, K. D. (2004). "Olfactory information processing in honeybee (*Apis mellifera*), nestmate recognition." *Animal Behaviour* 68, 921–928.

Cao, T. T., Hyland, K. M., Malechuk, A., Lewis, L. A., and Schneider, S.S. (2009). "The effect of repeated vibration signals on worker behavior in established and newly founded colonies of the honey bee, Apis mellifera." *Behavioral Ecology and Sociobiology* 63, 521–529.

D'Ettorre, P. D., Wenseleers, T., Dawson, J., Hutchinson, S., Boswell, T., and Ratnieks, F.L.W. (2006). "Wax combs mediate nestmate recognition by guard honeybees." *Animal Behaviour* 71, 773–779.

Dreller, C., and Tarpy, D. R. (2000). "Perception of the pollen need by foragers in a honeybee colony." *Animal Behaviour* 59, 91–96.

Dukas, R. (2008). "Life history of learning: Performance curves of honeybees in settings that minimize the role of learning." *Animal Behaviour* 75, 1125–1130.

———. (2008). "Life history of learning: Performance curves of honeybees in the wild." *Ethology* 114, 1195–1200.

Fewell, J. H. (2003). "Social insect networks." *Science* 301, 1867–1870.

Frisch, B., and Koeniger, N. (1994). "Social synchronization of the activity rhythms of honeybees within a colony." *Behavioral Ecology and Sociobiology* 35, 91–98.

Galizia, C. G. (2007). "Brainwashing, honeybee style." *Science* 317, 326–327.

Gilley, D. C. (2003). "Absence of nepotism in the harassment of dueling queens by honeybee workers." *Proceedings of the Royal Society of London* 270, 2045–2049.

Goulson, D., and Sparrow, K. R. (2009). "Evidence for competition between honeybees and bumblebees: Effects on bumblebee worker size." *Journal of Insect Conservation* 13, 177–181.

Hurd, L. (2000). "Health from the honeybee." *Total Health* 22, 54–56.

Johnson, B. R. (2002). "Organization of work in the honeybee: A compromise between division of labour and behavioural flexibility." *Proceedings of the Royal Society of London* 270, 147–152.

———. (2005). "Limited flexibility in temporal caste system of the honey bee." *Behavioral Ecology and Sociobiology* 58, 219–226.

———. (2008). "Global information sampling in the honey bee." *Naturwissenschaften* 95, 523–530.

Jones, J. C., Myerscough, M. R., Graham, S., and Oldroyd, B. P. (2004). "Honey bee nest thermoregulation: Diversity promotes stability." *Science* 305, 402–404.

Latty, T., Duncan, M., and Beekman, M. (2009). "High bee traffic disrupts transfer of directional information in flying honeybee swarms." *Animal Behaviour* 78, 117–121.

Leadbeater, E., and Chittka, L. (2007). "Social learning in insects—from miniature brains to consensus building." *Current Biology* 17, R703–R713.

Maderspacher, F. (2007). "All the queen's men." *Current Biology* 17, R191–R195.

Mattila, H. R., and Seeley, T. D. (2007). "Genetic diversity in honey bee colonies enhances productivity and fitness." *Science* 317, 362–364.

Menzel, R., and Giurfa, M. (2001). "Cognitive architecture of a mini-brain: The honeybee." *Trends in Cognitive Sciences* 5, 62–71.

Moore, D. (2001). "Honey bee circadian clocks: Behavioral control from individual workers to whole-colony rhythms." *Journal of Insect Physiology* 47, 843–857.

Moritz, R.F.A., and Kryger, P. (1994). "Self-organization of circadian rhythms in groups of honeybees." *Behavioral Ecology and Sociobiology* 34, 211–215.

Muller, H., and Chittka, L. (2008). "Animal personalities: The advantage of diversity." *Current Biology* 18, R961–R963.

Nakamura, J., and Seeley, T. D. (2006). "The functional organization of resin work in honeybee colonies." *Behavioral Ecology and Sociobiology* 60, 339–349.

O'Donnell, S., and Bulova, S. J. (2007). "Worker connectivity: A review of the design of worker communication systems and their effects on task performance in insect societies." *Insectes Sociaux* 54, 203–210.

Oldroyd, B. P. (2007). "What's killing American honey bees?" *PLoS Biology* 5, 1195–1199.

Oldroyd, B. P., and Fewell, J. H. (2008). "Large fitness benefits from polyandry in the honey bee." *Trends in Ecology and Evolution* 23, 59–60.

Oliver, R. (2007). "Fat bees—Part I." *American Bee Journal* 147, 714–718.

———. (2007). "Fat bees—Part II." *American Bee Journal* 147, 791–796.

Page, R. E., Jr., and Erber, J. (2002). "Levels of behavioral organization and the evolution of division of labor." *Naturwissenschaften* 89, 91–106.

Pankiw, T. (2007). "Brood pheromone modulation of pollen forager turnaround time in the honey bee." *Journal of Insect Behavior* 20, 173–180.

Passino, K. M., Seeley, T. D., and Visscher, P. K. (2008). "Swarm cognition in honey bees." *Behavioral Ecology and Sociobiology* 62, 401–414.

Peterson, I. (1999). "The honeycomb conjecture." *Science News* 156, 60–61.

Praini, D. R. (2004). "Impact of the introduced honey bee on native bees: A review." *Austral Ecology* 29, 399–407.

Pratt, S. C. (2004). "Collective control of the timing and type of comb construction by honey bees." *Apidologie* 35, 193–205.

Ratnieks, F.L.W., and Wenseleers, T. (2005). "Policing insect societies." *Science* 307, 54–56.

———. (2007). "Altruism in insect societies and beyond: Voluntary or enforced?" *Trends in Ecology and Evolution* 23, 45–52.

Rivera-Marchand, B., Giray, T., and Guzmán-Novoa, E. (2008). "The cost of defense in social insects: insights from the honey bee." *Entomologia Experimentalis et Applicata* 129, 1–10.

Robinson, G. E. (1984). "Worker and queen honey bee behavior during foreign queen introduction." *Insectes Sociaux* 31, 254–263.

———. (1998). "From society to genes with the honey bee." *American Scientist* 86, 456–462.

Rueppell, O., Bachelier, C., Fondrik, M. K., and Page, R. E. (2007). "Regulation of life history determines lifespan of worker honey bees (*Apis mellifera* L.)." *Experimental Gerontology* 42, 1020–1032.

Sagili, R. R., and Pankiw, T. (2007). "Effects of protein-constrained brood food on honey bee pollen foraging and colony growth." *Behavioral Ecology and Sociobiology* 61, 1471–1478.

Scheiner, R., Page, R. E., and Erber, J. (2004). "Sucrose responsiveness and behavioral plasticity in honey bees (*Apis mellifera*)." *Apidologie* 35, 133–142.

Schmickl, T., and Crailsheim, K. (2001). "Cannibalism and early capping: Strategy of honeybee colonies in times of experimental pollen shortages." *Journal of Comparative Physiology (A)* 187, 541–547.

———. (2004). "Costs of environmental fluctuations and benefits of dynamic decentralized foraging decisions in honey bees." *Adaptive Behavior* 12, 263–277.

Schmid-Hempel, P., and Wolf, T. (1988). "Foraging effort and lifespan of workers in a social insect." *Journal of Animal Ecology* 57, 500–521.

Schneider, S. S., and DeGrandi-Hoffman, G. (2008). "Queen replacement in African and European honey bee colonies with and without afterswarms." *Insectes Sociaux* 55, 79–85.

Schulz, D. J., Huang, Z., and Robinson, G. E. (1998). "Effects of colony food shortage on behavioral development in honey bees." *Behavioral Ecology and Sociobiology* 42, 295–303.

Seeley, T. D. (1997). "Honey bee colonies are group-level adaptive units." *American Naturalist* 150 (supplement), 522–541.

Seeley, T. D., and Visscher, P. K. (2003). "Choosing a home: How the scouts in a honey bee swarm perceive the completion of their group decision making." *Behavioral Ecology and Sociobiology* 54, 511–520.

Seeley, T. D., Visscher, P. K., and Passino, K. M. (2006). "Group decision making in honey bee swarms." *American Scientist* 94, 220–229.

Sharma, V. K., and Chandrashekaran, M. K. (2005). "Zeitgebers (time cues) for biological clocks." *Current Science* 89, 1136–1146.

Sherman, G., and Visscher, P. K. (2002). "Honeybee colonies achieve fitness through dancing." *Nature* 419, 920–922.

Slessor, K. N., Winston, M. L., and LeConte, Y. (2005). "Pheromone communication in the honeybee." *Journal of Chemical Ecology* 31, 2731–2745.

Sumpter, D.J.T. (2006). "The principles of collective animal behaviour." *Philosophic Transactions of the Royal Society (B)* 361, 5–22.

Tanner, D., and Visscher, K. (2008). "Does the body orientation of waggle dance followers affect the accuracy of recruitment?" *Apidologie* 40, 55–62.

Tarpy, D. R., Gilley, D. C., and Seeley, T. D. (2004). "Levels of selection in a social insect: A review of conflict and cooperation during honey bee queen replacement." *Behavioral Ecology and Sociobiology* 55, 513–523.

Viuda-Martos, M., Ruiz-Navajas, Y., Fernández-López, J., and Pérez-Álvarez, J. A. (2008). "Functional properties of honey, propolis, and royal jelly." *Journal of Food Science* 73, R117–R124.

Wei, C. A., and Dyer, F. C. (2009). "Investing in learning: Why do honeybees, *Apis mellifera*, vary the durations of learning flights?" *Animal Behaviour* 77, 1165–1177.

Weidenmüller, A., and Tautz, J. (2002). "In-hive behavior of pollen foragers in honey bee colonies under conditions of high and low pollen need." *Ethology* 108, 205–221.

Weinstock, M. (2006). "Self-organization and material constructions." *Architectural Design* 76, 34–41.

Wolf, T. J., and Schmid-Hempel, P. (1989). "Extra loads and foraging life span in honeybee workers." *Journal of Animal Ecology* 58, 943–954.

Woyciechowski, M., and Moron, D. (2009). "Life expectancy and onset of foraging in the honeybee (*Apis mellifera*)." *Insectes Sociaux* 56, 193–201.

Wray, M. K., Klein, B. A., Mattila, H. R., and Seeley, T. D. (2008). "Honeybees do not reject dances for 'implausible' locations: Reconsidering the evidence for cognitive maps in insects." *Animal Behaviour* 76, 261–269.

Zhang, S., Bock, F., Si, A., Tautz, J., and Srinivasan, M. V. (2005). "Visual working memory in decision making by honey bees." *PNAS* 102, 5250–5255.

Zhang, S., Schwarz, S., Pahl, M., Zhu, H., and Tautz, J. (2006). "Honeybee memory: A honeybee knows what to do and when." *Journal of Experimental Biology* 209, 4420–4428.

Magazines and Newspapers

BusinessWeek (3/9/2009). "Cutting Costs Without Cutting Jobs." By Matthew Boyle and Frederik Balfour.

—— (5/11/2009). "The Art of Succession." By Matthew Boyle.

—— (8/17/2009). "Howard Schultz Versus Howard Schultz." By Susan Berfield.

——. (11/02/2009). "Risky Business at Nissan." By David Welch and Ian Rowley.

Chief Executive (April/May 2007). "The Art of the Deal: Integration Strategies That Work." By C. J. Prince, Gerald Adolph, and J. Neely.

Economist (8/11/2007). "Will She, Won't She?"

—— (2/28/2009). "Managing in the Fog."

——. (10/10/2009). "A Young Town Again."

Financial Times (12/2/2008). "The Chaos Theory of Leadership." By Peter Marsh and Stefan Stern.

—— (4/6/2009). "Monday Interview—John Lechleiter: A Pharma Leader Who Thinks Long." By Andrew Jack.

—— (11/09/2009). Monday Interview—"Peter Löscher: The Team Player at the Top." By Daniel Schäfer.

—— (4/30/2009). "Female Talent Takes to the Boards." By Alison Maitland.

—— (7/21/2009). "Time Out to Help Less Fortunate Is Its Own Reward." By Rhymer Rigby.

Fortune (5/31/2004). "The Real Story." By Betsy Morris, Patricia Sellers, Julie Schlosser, Ellen Florian, John Helyar, and Patricia Neering.

—— (2/2/2009). "Steve's Leave: What Does It Really Mean?" By Adam Lashinsky.

—— (4/27/2009). "Yahoo's Taskmaster." By Jon Fortt.

—— (8/31/2009). "Pfizer's Home Remedy." By Alyssa Abkowitz.

Harvard Business Review (6/2007). "Help Newly Hired Executives Adapt Quickly." By Michael Watkins.

New York Times (4/04/1960). Personal communication from Fred Shapiro, author of The Yale Book of Quotations.

—— (4/7/2009). "After Recession, Recovery Will Take Years." By Louis Uchitelle.

—— (5/10/2009). "Backlash: Women Bullying Women." By Mickey Meece.

—— (8/18/2009). "Brain Is a Co-conspirator in a Vicious Stress Loop." By Natalie Angier.

——— (11/12/2009). "Hewlett-Packard to Acquire 3Com." By Steve Lohr.

New York Times Magazine (7/26/2009). "The New Joblessness." By Roger Lowenstein.

Pittsburgh Post-Gazette (7/12/2009). "Editorial: Vintage LCB Rube Goldberg Would Like Kiosk Plan to Sell Wine."

Wall Street Journal (1/21/2009). "Executive Education: A Female Face on Executive M.B.A.s—Business Schools Step Up Efforts to Attract More Women to Pricey Degree." By Alina Dizik.

——— (3/23/2009). "P&G's Lafley Sees CEOs as Link to World." By Ellen Byron.

——— (3/26/2009). "Zara Grows as Retail Rivals Struggle." By Cecilie Rohwedder.

——— (4/6/2009). "R&D Spending Holds Steady in Slump—Big Companies Invest to Grab Sales in Recovery; the iPod Lesson." By Justin Scheck and Paul Glader.

——— (5/14/2009). "Commuter Carrier Flies for Three Big Airlines." By Susan Carey.

——— (5/18/2009). "Railway Keeps Its Furloughed at Hand." By Alex Roth.

——— (6/22/2009). "In Search of Innovation." By John Bessant, Kathrin Moslein, and Bettina von Stamm.

——— (8/11/2009). "The Game: The Two Sides of Verizon's Deal Making." By Dennis K. Berman.

——— (8/18/2009). "Vegetable Gardens Help Morale Grow." By Raymund Flandez.

———— (09/28/2009). "Top Small Workplaces 2009." By Kelly K. Spors.

———— (11/21/2009). "BofA's Lewis May Consider Postponing Retirement." By Dan Fitzpatrick.

Wired (August 2009). "Your Future in 5 Easy Steps: *Wired* Guide to Personal Scenario Planning." By Peter Schwartz.